Woodirons

Woodirons

Thomas Kiernan

Photography by Jean Brind

Prentice-Hall, Inc., Englewood Cliffs, New Jersey 07632

Woodirons by Thomas Kiernan
Copyright © 1981 by Thomas Kiernan

Address inquiries to Prentice-Hall, Inc.,
Englewood Cliffs, N. J. 07632
Printed in the United States of America
Prentice-Hall International, Inc., London
Prentice-Hall of Australia, Pty. Ltd., Sydney
Prentice-Hall of Canada, Ltd., Toronto
Prentice-Hall of India Private Ltd., New Delhi
Prentice-Hall of Japan, Inc., Tokyo
Prentice-Hall of Southeast Asia Pte. Ltd., Singapore
Whitehall Books Limited, Wellington, New Zealand
10   9   8   7   6   5   4   3   2   1

Library of Congress Cataloging in Publication Data

Kiernan, Thomas.
    Woodirons.

    1. Golf.   I. Title.
GV965.K48   796.352'3   81-12091
                                              AACR2
ISBN 0-13-962506-2

Introduction

Scores of books and countless magazine articles have been written over the past several decades devoted to teaching you how to improve your golf game. Some, authored by well-known professionals, have concentrated on revamping your basic golfing style and technique—grip, stance, swing, and so on. Others have simply been collections of tips designed to help you overcome specific weaknesses. Still others have been highly esoteric technical manuals filled with complex graphs and charts illustrating abstract data concerning swing arcs, body kinetics, hand dynamics, and similar concepts. The likelihood is that if any of these books and articles have bettered your game, the improvement has been marginal at best.

Why, then, another book promising radically to improve your golf game when so many previous books have failed?

The answer: because this book is not a conventional teaching book. It does not require you to make wholesale changes in your golfing techniques—techniques that undoubtedly, over years of playing, you have become well accustomed to. Indeed, the book encourages you to acknowledge that it is your less-than-perfect technique that prevents you from playing the golf you wish you could play. It then offers you a method by which you can bypass that technical barrier.

I call it the Woodiron Method.

As you will learn in more detail in the pages ahead, the vast majority of recreational golfers, men and women, fail to play up to their potential primarily because, for various reasons having to do with swing technique and mental outlook, they cannot use their irons consistently or well. If you have picked up this book, you are most likely such a golfer—a golfer whose handicap is much higher than it would be if only you were able to master the iron game. Yet you know that to gain any proficiency with your irons would demand a radical alteration in your basic golfing technique—an alteration both expensive in the lessons it requires and time-consuming in the practice it entails.

The Woodiron Method of golf provides you with a cheaper,

faster, and more efficient way to become a good iron player, and thereby to significantly reduce your handicap and increase the pleasure you get out of golf. The Woodiron Method means, simply, playing golf with wood clubs instead of conventional irons—wood clubs that are designed and engineered to function like irons but "feel" and play like regular woods.

The method is proving highly beneficial to an increasing number of golfers who have labored in vain for years to improve their conventional-iron game. If you are among the millions of golfers whose improvement and pleasure have been inevitably frustrated by their inability to play with the irons on a consistent and effective basis, the Woodiron Method offers you a means to overcome your frustration quickly, easily, and at a small expense.

The purposes of this book, then, are to introduce you to the Woodiron Method, to show how it can markedly improve your game over a period of just a few days, and to provide a special program by which you can best make the transition from irons to woodirons, should you decide to do so.

Naturally, I hope you do so decide, since I believe the Woodiron Method will vastly increase the satisfaction and pleasure the game of golf is capable of giving you.

Contents

The "iron syndrome"

According to statistics, of the 21 million American men who play recreational golf regularly, 67 per cent labor under handicaps of 20 and more. Of the remaining 33 per cent, well over half are in the 15-to-20 handicap range. Of that remainder, well over half are in the 10-to-15 range. Only 4 per cent of all male golfers play to handicaps of 9 or less.

The figures for women are comparable. About 6 million women play golf regularly—that is, at least once a week during a season. Seventy-three per cent play to handicaps of 20 or more. Of the remaining 27 per cent, almost three quarters are in the 15-to-20 range. Of the remaining 8 per cent, another three quarters play between 10 and 15. Only 2 per cent of all women golfers are capable of playing at handicaps of 10 or less.

An excellent-to-good golfer, male or female, is defined by the United States Golf Association as one who plays to a handicap of between 1 and 9. A good-to-average golfer is one who plays between 10 and 16. An average-to-below-average player is one whose handicap is between 16 and 22. And a poor golfer, or duffer, is anyone who plays at a handicap that exceeds 22.

Using the foregoing figures, it is safe to say that we are a nation of duffers. The question is, why? The answers are many.

One is that the ordinary American golfer does not practice or play enough. Another is that the basic golf swing is an intensely athletic maneuver demanding a high degree of physical coordination and timing, and the average American does not possess the innate athletic gifts to execute it properly. A third has to do with psychology and temperament. Every golf shot requires a concentrated but cool, relaxed, even detached mental approach to its physical execution. Most Americans are incapable of maintaining such states of mind and emotion in the face of the problems presented by every golf shot.

These answers are undoubtedly true so far as they go. But a more profound explanation underlies them all. It embraces both the physical *and* the mental failings of most golfers, and it is reflected in another body of statistics.

In 1978 a golfing magazine conducted a survey of 247 teaching professionals around the country. The pros were asked to analyze and describe the five weakest elements in the average recreational player's game, handicap notwithstanding. (Putting and sand trap play were excluded.)

The results of the poll showed that, in the estimation of the teaching pros, the weakest factor in the average golfer's game was in the long irons (2, 3, and 4). That is, the hardest shots for anyone to execute properly and consistently were the long-iron shots.

The second most common weakness of the recreational golfer—good, average, and poor alike—resided in the mid-iron game (5, 6, and 7).

The third weakest aspect lay with the short irons (8, 9, and 10, or pitching wedge).

The fourth was ascribed to the fairway woods and the fifth to the driver.

What does the poll reveal? According to one of the pros who participated:

Here we have a vivid profile of the greatest difficulties that confront every golfer between tee and green. The old axiom that success or failure in golf depends on one's ability with the putter is only partly true. For the golfer who can consistently reach the green in regulation, the putter, of course, becomes the vital club. But so many golfers get themselves hung up between tee and green that by the time they're on

*the putting surface, their skill with the putter is only incidental to their
score.*

*A good tee-to-green golfer who can't putt well may end up
missing a few makable birdies and will even accumulate a few
bogeys, which is frustrating. But far more frustrating and discour-
aging is constantly making bogeys, double bogeys, and triple bogeys—
all because you have trouble getting on the green in the first place.
This is the problem for most high-handicap golfers, and it stems
directly from the fact that they have so much difficulty maneuvering
the ball onto the green, after the tee shot, in regulation.*

*After observing thousands of golfers, I can say that the difficulty
comes primarily from the cold, hard fact that they can't play the iron
game the way it's supposed to be played.*

In preparing this book, I interviewed professionals at more
than thirty golf courses in the Northeast and California. To a man
they agreed with the survey pro's analysis. Said one, pointing to a
club member waiting to tee off for a round in a weekend tournament:

*Mr. Henderson over there is an example of your average mid-to-high-
handicap twice-a-week golfer. Last time I looked he was playing with
a 21 or 22. I can predict what his round today will be like. Let's start
with this opening hole. It's a 410-yard par 4 with a slight downhill
dogleg to the left. Henderson's strong, and he'll hit a drive of about
220 yards. But it'll fade a bit, so that, although it'll clear the bend in
the fairway, which is about 190 yards out, the ball will end up in the
low rough along the right side of the fairway. He'll be about 210 yards
from the stick instead of 190 if he'd been able to draw the ball a little
or driven straight down the middle left.*

*Now if a top-notch golfer hits that drive, it's a poor tee shot for
him. But it's salvageable—that is, he can still reach the green from
where he lies with a 2 or 3 iron. Because the rough is fairly stubbly out
there and the ball isn't going to be sitting up for a nice wood shot,
Henderson is going to have to use a long iron to get out. He can't hope
to reach the green on the fly with a long iron, but he'll figure that if he
can get a good straight shot, he'll get enough distance to land the ball
in front of the green on the downhill slope and roll it on. But the
trouble with that thinking is that he really can't handle a 2 or 3 iron
very well, even from a nice fairway lie. So what's going to happen is*

that he'll probably scuttle the ball out of there. It'll start off in the general direction of the green on a low trajectory, but then it'll skew offline to the right or left. Since he's going downhill, he'll get a little roll when the ball lands, but he'll leave himself 50 to 80 yards away from the green and off the fairway, so that he's still shooting from the rough. Not only that, but because he's off to the side he'll have to loft his next shot over one of the traps that protect the side of the green. That shot calls for a wedge or 9 iron, and a top golfer would give it a nice cut so that it holds the green. Henderson will probably use an 8, but again, because he has no touch, the shot will fail. He's looking at the trap he has to get over and still hold the green because there's a trap on the other side, and all this time he's going to be thinking. What he's going to be thinking about is that he doesn't know whether he has the finesse to pull the shot off. Finally he'll play the shot, but his doubts and uncertainties will be built right into his swing and he'll have absolutely no control over what happens. If he's lucky, the ball will go straight with the right distance and it'll hit the green and hold within two-putt range. But golfers like Henderson only have so much luck in them.

What's more likely to happen is that he'll make his swing tentative and hit the ball short, into the near trap. Or else he'll slice or shank it offline and still be well off the green, shooting 4. Maybe he'll finally get on in four and two-putt for a 6. That's about his best possibility. But, you see, he's started off with a double bogey and that's more or less how his whole round will go. No birdies, maybe a lucky par or two, and lots of bogeys and double bogeys. Why? Because his irons will always be getting him into trouble. Whether he's hitting a long iron to recover from a mediocre drive, or a mid- or short iron as an approach shot to the green, or a long to mid-iron off a par-3 tee, he's going to create more problems for himself than he solves. Henderson's a fairly decent putter, so that's not his problem; in fact, his putting keeps his handicap from being four or five digits higher. And his woods are okay, even off the tee—I mean, his woods generally don't get him into serious trouble. At worst he might put an occasional drive into the rough alongside the fairway. For a good iron player, this presents nothing more than a routine second shot. But Henderson, like most golfers, cannot handle the long and mid-irons with any consistency or confidence, and he's not even that hot with the short irons. And that's where most golfers have their greatest problems— after their drive and before they can start putting.

   Now a lot of guys will tell you that their problems always crop up when they're close to the green—playing out of bunkers or out of the rough around the green to get on the putting surface, or else hitting precision-pitch shots from a short distance out to get close to the pin. When they say that, I always tell them: wait a minute, why did you get into that trap or rough in the first place? Sure, you're being forced to play trouble shots when you're close to the green, but what created the trouble to begin with? And of course it was their long and mid-iron approach shots. That's why they're always being forced to take two, three extra shots per hole. Eighty-five per cent of it is due to the fact that they can't play the long and mid-irons.

   Why are irons the greatest bugaboo of most golfers? When I put the question to a group of other pros, the answer was invariably the same in substance: of the three basic clubs in golf, irons provide the least margin for error, and the margin is progressively reduced as one descends the scale from 10 iron to 1 iron. Also, the swing required for iron shots is different from the swing the average recreational golfer envisions as the natural golf swing—the wood swing.

   Too, consider this: the average par-4 golf hole is 355 yards in length. This means that given the average drive of 200 yards, the representative golfer's second shot always calls for a long to mid-iron. The average par-5 hole measures 450 yards in length. This means that the golfer's third shot calls for a mid- to short iron. And the average par-3 hole is 135 yards long. Which means that the golfer's tee shot always calls for a long to mid-iron. Thus, over the course of an average 18 holes, a long-, mid-, or short-iron shot is called for at least 18 times. Studies have shown that a scratch golfer will utilize his irons on an average of 23 occasions when shooting a round of par (this includes sand play and other trouble situations). The same studies reveal that a 15-handicap golfer will employ his irons 51 times when shooting a round equivalent to his handicap—well over twice as often as the scratch golfer. And a 30-handicapper will use his irons with proportionately greater frequency.

Indeed, the studies show, it is the more frequent *need* to use the irons that inflates golf scores. Frequency of iron use is a direct measure of a golfer's handicap. Put simply, the more you need to use an iron, the less capable you are. Perversely, it is your very inability to play irons correctly that leads to their higher frequency of use during a given round of golf.

By way of proving this point, in the summer of 1980 I put together a series of golf rounds with thirty male golfers of varying abilities. Ten were players with handicaps of between 3 and 8—low-handicap golfers. Ten played to handicaps of between 13 and 18—mid-handicappers. And ten were high-handicap golfers, each carrying a handicap of 25 or more. I formed ten threesomes, each made up of a golfer from each handicap category, and sent them out to play a round on a par-72 course in my area. I charted each round, keeping track of each player's every shot and club used. When the ten threesomes were finished I fed all the data I had accumulated into a bank's computer. The computer came up with a model of all thirty golfers' rounds. Here is how the computerized stroking went for each of the three representative handicap categories in a typical threesome on a computer-model par-3 hole, par-4 hole, and par-5 hole. If you follow the descriptions carefuly, you will learn a lot about your own golfing patterns.

The representative par-3 hole was 153 yards long. Its fairly large, flat, slightly elevated green was fronted by a medium-sized pond and bounded laterally and at the rear by three medium-deep traps. The terrain extending from the outer edges of the lateral traps sloped downward fairly steeply to groves of trees about 50 yards from the pin. The pin was set in the right-center portion of the green as viewed from the tee. *(See Fig. 1.)*

(1) The Low-Handicap Golfer: Hit *tee shot* with a 6 iron: ball landed on forward part of green and rolled to center, coming to stop hole-high but 18 feet from cup. Left first putt short by a foot, holed out in a par.

(2) The Mid-Handicap Golfer: Hit *tee shot* with a 5 iron: ball pulled left, missing green and left-hand trap entirely; ball landed on shoulder next to trap, trickled down slope, and stopped in rough

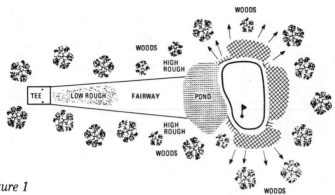

Figure 1

next to tree line, 50 yards from pin. Hit *second shot* with a pitching wedge (10 iron): ball fell short into trap. Hit *third shot* with sand wedge: ball barely got onto green, stopping 45 feet from cup. Two putts, however, salvaged a double-bogey 5.

(3) The High-Handicap Golfer: Hit *tee shot* with a 4 iron: anxious to ensure that he'd carry pond, he overswung and skulled the ball into water 100 yards away. Dropped a new ball at rear of pond for penalty and attempted his *third shot*, 40 yards across pond to the right side of green, with a 9 iron: ball drifted too far right and settled in right-hand trap. *Fourth shot* was a blast that caught too much of ball and sent it to fringe of trap on the other side of the green. *Fifth shot* was a chip that stopped 10 feet from cup. Two putts for a quadruple-bogey 7.

Here's how the stroking went on the computer-modeled par 4, a straight, slightly downhill hole of 415 yards with two shallow traps bordering the fairway 210 yards from the tee to catch errant drives, a brook guarding the front of the green, and three traps encircling it. *(See Figure. 2)*

(1) The Low-Handicap Golfer: Hit *tee shot* with a driver: ball carried 230 yards in the air, clearing right-hand fairway trap, and bounced another 15 yards to settle in right rough (total yardage of drive: 245). Lying 170 yards from green, hit *second shot* with a 3

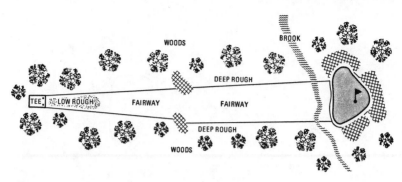

Figure 2

iron: ball pulled slightly left, cleared brook, and came to rest on grass fringe between green and left-hand trap, about 50 feet from flag. *Third shot,* a delicate running chip with a 6 iron, left ball 3 feet from cup. Missed first putt by inches and holed out for a bogey 5.

(2) The Mid-Handicap Golfer: Hit *tee shot* with a driver: ball traveled straight and bold for 200 yards, splitting fairway traps and rolling another 30 yards for a total yardage of 230. Lying 185 yards from green and 170 from fronting brook, was afraid to try a wood shot for fear of not reaching green and catching brook; instead hit *second shot* with a 5 iron, hoping to lay up before brook and set up an easy chip to green: ball skewed offline to the right, however, and came to stop in rough off right side of fairway about 30 yards in front of brook. *Third shot* called for golfer to loft the ball nearly 60 yards across brook and then over edge of right-hand trap to reach green; *hit shot* with a 9 iron: ball fell short into trap. Hit *fourth shot* into bank of trap and needed a *fifth shot* to get onto green. Two putts gave him a triple-bogey 7.

(3) The High-Handicap Golfer: Hit *tee shot* with a driver: ball hooked left and rolled into shallow fairway trap. Hit *second shot* with a 5 iron, also planning to lay up in front of brook: skulled ball, bouncing it off front lip of trap so that it came to rest in fairway but still 150 yards from green. Hit *third shot* with a 4 iron, going for green: ball pulled left, getting over brook but ending up on hardpan at edge of tree line, 40 yards from pin with the left-hand trap

intervening. Hit *fourth shot* with a 9 iron: ball flew over trap into bunker on opposite side of green. Blasted onto green with *fifth shot*, but stopped 60 feet short of cup. Needed three putts to get down for a quadruple-bogey 7.

And here's how it went on the 510-yard par-5 hole, which doglegged sharply to the right 200 yards out, had a large trap set at the crook of the bend to catch sliced drives, a further group of traps intruding on the narrowing fairway to gobble up feeble second shots, a shallow trap guarding the front of the rightward down-sloping green, a huge, yawning bunker at back, and a steep, rough-encrusted fall-off bank along the right side of the green. *See Fig. 3.)*

(1) The Low-Handicap Golfer: Hit *tee shot* with a driver: struck a tremendous drive that carried the bend and rolled to a stop at far edge of fairway, 260 yards from tee and 180 yards from fairway traps ahead. Hit *second shot* with a 3-wood: ball carried straight over traps and stopped 30 yards in front of trap guarding front of green. Hit *third shot* with a 10 iron, nicely clearing guard trap and bouncing ball to a stop within 4 feet of pin. One-putted for a birdie 4.

(2) The Mid-Handicap Golfer: Hit *tee shot* with a driver: ball went straight and just cleared bend, coming to rest in fairway 210 yards from tee and 230 yards from fairway traps ahead. Hit *second shot* with a 3 wood: planning to lay up before fairway traps, he succeeded, his ball coming to rest 30 yards in front of traps and 120 yards from green. Hit *third shot* with a 7 iron: plenty of distance, but ball faded sharply right to hit steep bank on right side of green, bounding down hill to a stop in rough 40 yards from elevated putting surface. Hit *fourth shot* with a 9 iron: ball, struck fat, failed to clear top of bank on right side of green; instead bounced back down off bank, leaving golfer still 25 yards away. Hit *fifth* shot out of deep rough with a sand wedge: ball landed on green 35 feet from cup. Two putts for a double-bogey 7.

(3) The High-Handicap Golfer: Hit *tee shot* with a driver: ball went straight but carried only 195 yards, not quite making dogleg bend and not giving golfer a clear second shot down fairway. Hit

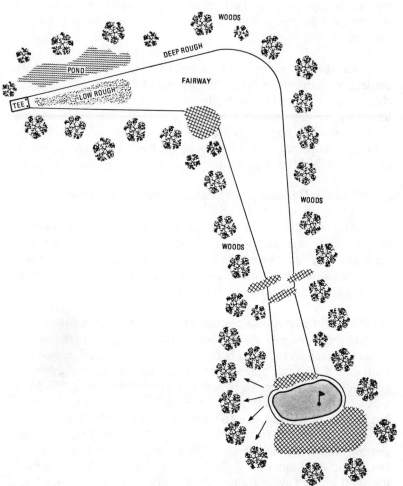

Figure 3

second shot with a 3 wood: ball faded nicely around bend and, traveling 170 yards, came to rest on right side of fairway—140 yards from edge of green and 60 yards from fairway traps. Hit *third shot* with a 5 iron, hoping to carry front guard trap and land squarely on green: ball, hit perfectly for a change, carried too far, however; it bounced off back edge of green and into deep, gaping crater trap at rear. Took two shots to get out of trap and two putts to get down for a double-bogey 7 on the relatively easy par 5.

What is the most compelling lesson of this computer analysis? Simply that the irons are what usually lead to the less than top-notch golfer's downfall on any given hole in any given round of golf. You'll notice that on each of the computer-sample holes, the mid-handicap and high-handicap players' troubles invariably started once they played their first iron shots; and that once in trouble, they only compounded their woes with further short-iron trouble shots. Had either of the golfers been able to play their irons with as much relative efficiency and consistency as they did their drivers and fairway woods, they would not have gotten into the difficulties they did, which led to still further miseries before they could find the cup.

The lesson is so clear, and the earlier corollary observations of teaching pros so unanimous, that they can be stated in the form of a law:

The higher a golfer's handicap, the more difficulty he or she has executing iron shots consistently.

Or to put it another way:

The ability of any golfer to improve his game is in direct proportion to his ability to master the irons.

But mastering the irons, as most golfers will agree, is probably the hardest thing to do in golf. Thus the ordinary golfer is left in a Catch-22 situation. As one well-known club pro says:

Drivers and fairway woods are relatively "low-skill" clubs. By that I mean almost any golfer can naturally get the ball up and away with them. Even if it doesn't always go straight, they'll get distance simply

*by giving the ball a good swipe. But irons are "high-skill" clubs, and
the lower the iron the more skill is needed. In the first place, the swing
is different. In the second, there's a lot less mass applied to the ball
than there is with a wood. You've got to strike an iron just about
perfectly to get the shot it's designed for. With a wood you can get
away with much less than a perfect hit and still end a good distance
toward the hole. Not so with an iron. Because you're dealing with
more precise distances, directions, and trajectories when you're confronted by a natural iron shot, and with targeting and finesse, the
tolerances are much lower than when you're setting up to play a
natural wood shot. When the average golfer plays a wood, whether
off the tee or as a fairway shot, all he's basically interested in is
getting as much distance as possible and a reasonable degree of direction. But when he is close enough to the green that his woods are of
no use—anywhere from 230 yards and in depending on the golfer—
the nature of the game changes abruptly. This is the nitty-gritty phase
of golf—the key-shot approach to the green. It's here that a golfer's
handicap is really established. And it's here that the average mid-to-
high-handicap golfer meets his Armageddon, usually. I've seen it
happen time and time again, even among golfers with low handicaps.
When a breakdown occurs, it is generally on the approach with an
iron. For example, on an average par-4 hole a good golfer, even a
mediocre golfer, will usually hit a drive that will put him into green-
reachable range with an iron—say, anywhere from 150 to 200 yards
out, depending on the drive's length. But now he's confronted by a
high-skill shot either to get on in regulation or close enough to
realistically maintain his chance of making a par. That means getting
close enough for an easy chip and a one-putt, not getting himself hung
up in the usual hazards that surround a green. To achieve this he has
to play anything from a 2 iron to a 7 iron, depending on the distance
and his natural power and the circumstances of the hole and weather.
He needs loft, and he needs the right direction and distance down to a
few yards' tolerance all around. Touring pros, club pros, most top
amateurs—this is a shot they can handle consistently. Anyone else—
well, it's a problematic deal, and most likely they'll flub the shot in
some way so as to guarantee no chance of making a par. Either they'll
hit it way too short or way offline or both, or else they'll put the ball
into trouble up near the green. Either way they're in trouble. I'd say*

the average golfer makes trouble for himself about 15 per cent of the time off the tee or fairway with a shot that calls for a wood. The other 85 per cent is the trouble they get into as a result of the shots that call for irons on approach. It's like flying. Very few planes crash on takeoff. Most crashes occur on approach to landing.

Why this collapse when it comes to irons? I put the question to several golf-playing psychiatrists of my acquaintance. The consensus, as one of them voiced it, was that:

It's largely psychological. The irons, especially the long and mid-irons, have a look and feel to them that seem alien to the golfer's task. Woods have bulky heads, large hitting surfaces, long and flexible shafts—all components that seem well geared to propelling a golf ball from a stationary position on the ground. A golfer holds a wood in his hands, he looks down and sees this good-sized clubhead, he settles it behind the ball and he thinks, "How can I miss?" Then put an iron in his hands. It's stiffer and shorter. But most of all it doesn't have a nice, large, comfortable club head at the end of it. Instead the golfer is now looking down at this thin, narrow blade, this wisp of steel, and the club bears no resemblance to what he thinks he needs to properly propel the golf ball. It's the blade, really; it spooks him because its minimal appearance is in stark contrast to the secure bulkiness of a wood's club head. He just knows by looking at it that the ball's going to be harder to hit properly. And then, when he tries it, all his fears are confirmed. He learns that it needs a different swing than the natural, sweeping wood swing he thinks is right—that it demands a much greater degree of precision at the impact moment, that it's much less forgiving than a wood. Once this reality becomes etched in his mind, he loses all confidence in his ability to hit with the iron. It's a constant source of anxiety to him and he comes to dread any shot that demands an iron. And of course that dread only serves to reinforce his fears and reconfirm his conviction that he can't use the club properly. The result is a further decline in his ability to execute iron shots with any consistency. It is what we psychiatrists, if we were treating golfers clinically, would call the "iron syndrome."

Why have I spent so much time in this opening chapter on the problems that irons pose? Because if you are the average mid-to-high-handicap golfer (10 and above), or even if you play at a handicap of under 10, it is most likely that you are a victim of the iron syndrome to one degree or another. I wanted to make you aware of how it works and why it works, and show you to what extent your irons are the Achilles' heel of your entire game, robbing you of the continuing pleasure and satisfaction you would experience if you could play golf consistently up to your physical and mental potential.

But I have another reason, too. And that is to let you know of a marvelous cure for the iron syndrome. It is called the Woodiron Method. If you have a handicap of 10 or more, and if you try it, you can reduce your handicap radically almost overnight. The rest of this book will be devoted to telling you what the Woodiron Method is and how you can best go about adopting it.

The woodiron method

The Woodiron Method did exactly that for me. It cut my handicap by almost half in less than a week. By throwing out my regular irons and replacing them with woodirons, I went from being a miserable 27-handicap hacker to a much happier 14-handicap golfer over the course of just five rounds of golf.

But I do not use myself as the sole basis for the virtues of the Woodiron Method. I have gotten to know scores of other golfers who have enjoyed similar if not better results after switching from irons to woodirons. Some I introduced to the method; others happened upon it themselves. But all have revolutionized both their games and their attitudes toward golf. For them a round of golf is no longer a source of unending frustration and self-disgust punctuated by occasional flashes of satisfaction at a rare well-played hole. Now satisfaction and pleasure are their dominant emotions as they play the game close to or on a par with their physical and mental potential. The muffed or errant shot has become the exception rather than the rule in their golfing lives. I have seen 12-handicappers go to handicaps of 5 or 6 in no time at all. I have seen 18-handicappers shrink to 7, 8, or 9 in a trice. I have seen 30-handicappers drop to 14 or 15 in as little as a week or so of regular playing. And I have seen duffers with handicaps so high they are beyond posting get down into the low 20s within a few weeks.

What did they all have in common? The fact that they replaced their conventional irons with what I call "woodirons."

What are woodirons? And what is the Woodiron Method?

Woodirons are golf clubs whose heads are made of wood and shaped like woods but whose hitting surfaces, or faces, are equivalent in loft to those of standard irons. The Woodiron Method is nothing more than playing golf with clubs made of wood instead of conventional steel.

Why does it work so well to improve the average golfer's game? Simply because woodirons, like the regular woods, provide a much greater margin of error and feel much more natural in the average golfer's hands than conventional irons.

In the pages ahead I am going to show you the best and quickest way to make the transition from irons to woodirons. I am not going to ask you to take my word blindly for the fact that woodirons can vastly improve your game. I am, however, going to ask you to give them a try and let the experiment, step by step, serve as its own proof. I am sure that very few of you, once you can gauge the results, will ever go back to conventional irons.

Woodirons were invented about forty years ago as "utility" clubs. The first such club was the 5 wood, which was the equivalent of the 1 iron in the loft angle of its club face. It proved to be a much more manageable club than the 1 iron in the hands of the ordinary golfer.

Two decades after the 5 wood arrived on the scene, custom club makers began to craft 6 and 7 woods to replace 2 and 3 irons in certain situations—mostly for the benefit of elderly golfers and weaker-hitting women. These too were considered utility woods. No self-respecting golfer would be seen with them in his bag; they were a symbol of weakness. The 5 wood gained quick acceptance, but it has only been within the past few years that interest in the 6 and 7 woods has spread. This was largely due to the fact that none other than top-earning pro Lee Trevino revealed that he had started using a 7 wood. (Indeed, at the 1980 U.S. Open at Baltusrol, Trevino announced that his 7 wood had been a key to his comeback from a two-year-long slump.)

Still, these "high-numbered" woods continued to be viewed as utility clubs in most quarters—to be used only in certain situations—

and were marketed as such by the handful of manufacturers who added them to their golf-club lines. But then there occurred a series of events in the life of a well-known amateur golfer from New Jersey named William "Billy" Dear.

From the nineteen-forties to the nineteen-sixties Billy Dear was one of the East's foremost amateur golfers, winning championships far and wide. He could easily have made a national name for himself as a touring pro in the era of Hogan and Snead. But because he was also a successful businessman, he decided to maintain his brilliant golfing career as an avocation.

In the late sixties Dear was seriously injured in an automobile accident. After twenty operations on his knees and hips, he returned to golf. But his once-scratch handicap was no more. The cause was his iron game. He found that the impact of irons against the turf reverberated throughout his body, sending lightning bolts of pain into his damaged joints. Soon he began to flinch with every iron shot. As his scores soared, his career as a top amateur seemed at an end. Even his doctors recommended that he give up golf. But he loved the game too much to follow their advice. Then he had an idea.

Dear had noticed that although his iron shots gave him acute discomfort, he could still execute wood shots without pain. This was because of the difference between the basic swings: proper iron shots demanded a descending jarring contact with the ground, whereas wood shots called for a sweeping swing that barely brushed the turf. Moreover, when a wood did contact the ground, much of the impact force was dissipated by the larger, more resilient club head. The club heads of irons—slender slabs of blunt steel—lacked the ability to dissipate impact forces; the forces traveled right up the shaft and through Dear's hands into his body.

Could irons made of wood instead of steel serve to alter this effect, Dear wondered? He went to a custom club maker and ordered a complete set of iron-equivalent woods, starting with a 5 wood—the equivalent of a 1 iron in club-face loft angle. A 6 wood, 7 wood, and 8 wood became replacements for his 2, 3, and 4 irons. A 9 wood, 10 wood, 11 wood, and 12 wood replaced his conventional 5, 6, 7 and 8 irons. Since 13 was an unlucky number, he skipped to a 14 wood to supplant his 9 iron and settled on a 15 wood to function as the equivalent of a pitching wedge.

When he received his new clubs, Dear worked with them briefly on the practice tee and discovered that they indeed did away with the pain of conventional iron shots. As he became more accustomed to them, he learned that he could execute just about any shot that called for an iron—long approaches, shots out of rough, medium pitches, short chips, sand shots, and short lofty cut shots over hazards. Not only that, but he could obtain the same pinpoint accuracy he had once been able to achieve with his regular irons. As he tells it, "The first time I used all woods was in 1970, in Florida, when I played a round with Arnold Palmer. He shot a 66, I shot a 69. He was amazed."

Over the course of a few rounds, Dear's handicap descended to scratch again. He proved that woodirons were a highly effective substitute for conventional irons in the hands of the golfer who has difficulty, for whatever reason, with conventional irons. "There's not a golfer I know, with the exception of a few top pros, whose game wouldn't improve if he switched to all woods instead of playing with irons," Dear says today. "The higher a player's handicap, the greater the improvement will be."

All this occurred more than ten years ago. Yet Dear's remarkable innovation went almost unnoticed by the golfing world. Only a handful of golf club manufacturers picked up on it and began to make sets of woodirons similar to the ones Billy Dear used. There was not much of a market for them, though. Still considered "utility" clubs and "freak" woods by the traditionalists, they were roundly shunned. As one club pro said at the time, "I won't stock them in my pro shop. You know those stores you see all over that sell aids for handicapped and lame people? Most of the members of this club are getting on in years, but they pride themselves on being able to still play golf. It wouldn't do for them to come into the pro shop and see these so-called woodirons displayed. It would make them feel as though I was selling aids to the handicapped. It would remind them of their age."

Unfortunately, that's the way woodirons were originally marketed—as clubs for golfers who were physically too feeble or debilitated to play with irons. A few years ago, I came across a set of woodirons on sale at a sporting-goods store. I had heard about Billy Dear, but it was the first time I had ever seen them and they fascinated me. I decided to buy a 14 wood—the equivalent of a pitching wedge—and give it a try. The result was no less than startling. All my golfing life I had had trouble executing accurate long and medium pitch shots to greens with any consistency. Over the course of a few rounds with the 14 wood, that glaring weakness in my game vanished almost completely. Using the 14 wood for shots that a professional golfer might use a sand wedge or pitching wedge to make, I suddenly found myself producing professional-type pitch shots of anywhere between 50 and 100 yards in length. The shots were the kind that would loft in picture-book fashion straight toward the green and settle firmly on the putting surface, more often than not within one-putt range of the hole.

The revelation of what I could do with a 14 wood, as compared to its iron equivalent, was overpowering. Since the rest of my iron repertoire was even worse than my ability with the pitching wedge, I went out and bought a 10 wood to test in place of my 6 iron. The 6 iron had been my usual club of choice for shots of about 160 yards. Now, instead of stroking an occasional good 6 iron while most of the time blowing the shot in one way or another, I was suddenly able to hit fine 6-iron shots time after time—with the 10 wood. It mattered not whether I was hitting from fairway or rough, from sand or tee; almost every shot I struck with my new 10 wood did what a well-executed 6-iron shot was supposed to do.

Once I started using the 14 wood and 10 wood, my handicap began to drop. And the pleasure I received from playing golf soared like a rocket. I couldn't wait to get more woodirons.

My next purchase was an 8 wood to use in place of my 4 iron. The results were happily similar: shots calling for a 4 iron became infinitely more steady and on the mark. I added a 9 wood and an 11 wood to replace my 5 and 7 irons, and again the improvement was remarkable. Finally, I simply threw out the rest of my irons and replaced them with woodiron equivalents.

Within a few weeks the contents of my golf bag looked like this:

Driver

3 wood

5 wood (1 iron equivalent)

6 wood (2 iron equivalent)

7 wood (3 iron equivalent)

8 wood (4 iron equivalent)

9 wood (5 iron equivalent)

10 wood (6 iron equivalent)

11 wood (7 iron equivalent)

12 wood (8 iron equivalent)

13 wood (9 iron equivalent)

14 wood (10 iron, or pitching wedge, equivalent)

Sand wedge

Putter

It was the legal maximum of 14 clubs. As I began to play regularly with an almost full bag of woods, I got stares of incredulity, sometimes hostility, from many other golfers. Then I received expressions of sympathy from some who assumed that because I was using "utility" clubs, I must be prematurely old or suffering from some crippling disease.

But I was neither old nor infirm. In my my mid-thirties at the time, I was strong and vigorous. I could hit a golf ball 250 yards with a driver and corresponding shorter distances with my conventional fairway woods. I was a fairly reliable putter. What had always been the nemeses of my game were the irons, I explained. I had found that by switching to woodirons, that handicap was to a large degree neutralized.

Few were impressed until they saw that my scores were rapidly, steadily shrinking. Then one golfer after another—usually players whose iron games weren't much better than mine—started to ask if they could try my new clubs. Soon bags full of woodirons became an increasingly common sight at my course. And other high handicaps began to shrink as my fellow players mastered the clubs.

But there remained a chorus of doubters. "They should be outlawed!" grumbled one traditionalist. "If you can't play golf with irons, you shouldn't play golf at all," said another. Both critics were also tennis players who had recently switched from conventional wooden rackets to oversized metal ones. When I reminded them of the contradiction in their attitudes, they got the point. Today both play golf with woodirons and are among their most avid proponents.

Speaking of getting the point, back in the early nineteen-seventies, after I had started using woodirons exclusively but was still receiving a lot of flak about their value, I set up an object-lesson demonstration over a period of several days for a group of mid- and high-handicap golfers at my course. There were twelve golfers in all, and all were skeptics. I sent each of them out for a round of golf with their own clubs. I walked the course with each golfer, trailing my own bag. The rules were that the golfer would play two balls—one using the clubs from his bag, the other using the woodiron clubs from my bag on any shot that normally called for an iron. I kept score for both balls, and advised on which number woodiron to use with the second ball.

None of the golfers had ever played with woodirons before, and only a few had tested them briefly on the practice tee. Yet, when the twelve double-ball rounds were completed, the results showed that all but one of the players had scored better with the second balls than with the first. The biggest differential was in the scores of one golfer who shot a 109 using his own irons with his first ball and a 92 using my woodirons with his second. The next biggest span was between a 102 on that golfer's first ball and an 89 on the second. The next was between a 98 and an 88. And so on. The eleventh golfer shot an 89 with his irons and an 85 with my woodirons. The only player who showed no improvement was a 2-handicapper, who scored a 75 on the par-72 course with his own clubs and a 75 with my woodirons.

But the point was proven. Eleven good-to-mediocre-to-poor golfers had scored well below their norm using woodirons, and without the benefit of having had a chance to play with the clubs before.

The point of my demonstration was well taken by most, and they immediately started using woodirons regularly. Today they still thank me for helping them forge such radical improvements in their games.

A few months later I conducted an identical experiment with eight women golfers whose handicaps ranged from 10 to beyond the moon. This time there was a marked improvement in *every* case. Even the 10-handicapper, who scored an 83 with her conventional irons, came in with a 79 using the woodirons.

Shortly after these demonstrations, word got around to a number of other golf courses in my area. I was approached by dozens of golfers, from my own course and elsewhere, to give lessons in the use of the woodirons. The informal teaching program I developed during that period serves as the basis for this book.

I should like to emphasize, however, that what I will be doing in the coming chapters is not so much a matter of teaching as it is of showing you how best and most quickly to adapt your game to the woodirons. I am not going to try to teach you how to play golf—the grip, the stance, the swing, and so on—because I am not a golf teacher and because, if you didn't already know how to play, you wouldn't be reading this book. Nor am I going to hector you about altering various components of your grip, stance, and swing techniques on the promise that such changes will improve your game. The beauty of woodirons is that you really don't have to change anything you do now, yet your game will automatically improve. All the Woodiron Method requires, basically, is an ability on your part to strike a golf ball with a conventional wood. If you can do that consistently—not always hitting the ball straight, necessarily, or far—you will find that woodirons will be of great benefit to you. This is particularly so if you, like most golfers, cannot strike irons as proficiently as you do your driver and fairway woods.

The other benefit of learning to play with woodirons is that they will improve your regular wood game as well. We have all heard more than once the primary rule of hitting a golf ball: "Let the club do the work." Probably the biggest problem all less than proficient golfers have is that they do not let their irons "do the work." Into almost every average golfer's iron swing is built extra "oomph." The result is usually a mis-hit. The same holds true when the average golfer attacks the ball with a driver or fairway wood. These woods are more forgiving, however, so the results are not always so disastrous. You may be offline, but at least you'll be out there.

The woodirons, once you become accustomed to their properties, do away with the urge to put extra "oomph" into your golf shots. Once you learn about the dynamics of the woodirons, once you experience how easily they "do the work," you will be much more inclined psychologically to hit your conventional wood shots similarly. I have found that most golfers not only improve their iron games by using woodirons, they also experience a marked improvement in their regular wood games—long tee shots, long fairway shots.

And none of this improvement requires uncomfortable changes in the way you are accustomed to swinging a golf club. Everyone has a grip, stance, and swing unique to himself or herself. Golfer A may have too short a backswing, golfer B too long a backswing. Golfer C may have too strong a grip, golfer D too weak. Golfer E may have too crouched a stance while golfer F's may be too upright.

It makes no difference. No matter what technical errors you may commit when you swing at a golf ball, it is *your* swing and you're stuck with it. Maybe because of your physical configuration, or because of a lack of natural physical coordination, or because of deeply ingrained swing habits, you will never be able to achieve the ideal swing mechanics. That's all right. With woodirons you don't need the ideal swing mechanics. All you need to be able to do is hit the ball with a wood. If you can do that, woodirons will effectively adapt themselves to your swing idiosyncrasies—certainly much more effectively than conventional irons do.

The key to the woodirons

The first woodiron I obtained was a replacement for the pitching wedge or 10 iron—the 14 wood. Later I learned that there was also available a 15 wood, which was the equivalent of the sand wedge. In due time I purchased one. I quickly discovered that this club was the key to learning the Woodiron Method. *(See Figs. 4 and 5.)*

Why? Because even more than the 14 wood, and certainly more than the sand wedge it replaces, the 15 wood has the greatest variety of effective functions. Its maximum range in distance is that of the sand wedge—say 125 yards for the strong golfer, 100 yards for the average golfer, 75 yards for the less strong golfer. So it is the club of choice for any straight, high approach shot to the green within these ranges.

But that's not all. The 15 wood can be used to great effect in a variety of other situations. It can be used efficiently to get onto the green from sand traps some distance from the green but still within the specified ranges. It can be used much more effectively than a steel wedge for pitch shots to the green from rough hardpan, or other bad lies. It is more consistent from all but the deepest bunkers around a green. And it's the most beneficial chipping tool I have ever encountered. Once you get the hang of it, you will find yourself using it for every kind of chip imaginable, from simple

Figure 4

Figure 5

unobstructed shots from the fringe of a green to lofted cut-shot chips over trees and embankments.

But there are two other reasons I call the 15 wood the key to the Woodiron Method. First, next to your putter, you will find that you will use the 15 wood more often than any other club in your bag during a given round of golf. Once you switch to woodirons, you will no longer view these clubs as utility clubs, least of all the 15 wood. Indeed, the 15 wood will become your bread-and-butter club, much more so than the conventional wedges are now.

Second, it is the 15 wood that will best give you the feel and touch of all the other woodirons. With the other woodirons, you will almost always take a full swing at the ball. You will swing full with the 15 wood too on occasion. But you will also find yourself executing shots with three-quarter swings, half swings, quarter swings, eighth swings, and even barely perceptible swings, using full grips, half-choke grips, and full-choke grips. Once you familiarize yourself with all the shots the 15 wood is capable of, you will have obtained an intimate feel for what the entire range of woodirons can do. And once you can strike the 15 wood consistently with a full swing—"letting the club do the work"—you will learn the precise distance every full shot will give you consistently. For some it may be 125 yards, for others 100 yards, for others only 75 yards. Whatever yardage you regularly get, that will be the measure of your use of the other woodirons. Finally, once you can hit the 15 wood straight and for consistent distances using a full swing, hitting the other woodirons with the same consistent direction, but for greater distances, will become second nature to you.

When I added the 15 wood to my bag, I wanted to keep my conventional sand wedge for dire emergencies, such as getting out of bottomless greenside bunkers or impossible lies. In order to obey the rule of golf that says that I could carry only 14 clubs, I removed my 6 wood. But soon I discovered that I needed a 6 wood on many more occasions than I needed my steel sand wedge. Indeed, in thirteen straight rounds of golf with both the 15 wood and sand wedge in my bag, I never once used the sand wedge. This was because the woodirons kept me out of the kind of trouble that my conventional irons used to get me into—trouble from which I could hope to recover only with a sand wedge.

Finally I put my 6 wood (2 iron) back in my bag and relegated my sand wedge to my attic. I can count on the fingers of both hands the times during the nine years thereafter that I was faced with a shot I could execute only with a sand wedge. Other than those, my 15 wood has served me to infinitely greater effect than my sand wedge ever did. Today I play with a full bag of woods, the only iron being my putter. Once you get the hang of the 15 wood's great variety, you will probably want to put away your sand iron too. *(See Fig. 6.)*

Before we get into the various techniques of the 15 wood, I will set out a chart for you to give you a clear idea of what you can expect in terms of distance from each of the woodirons, depending on your natural hitting power.

By "natural power" I mean the power you generate when you swing within yourself and impart optimum timing and rhythm to

Figure 6

your shot. This is not the power many golfers generate when they instinctively or deliberately try to "force" their shots. This power usually is destructive, upsetting timing and rhythm and causing an "overswing" that inevitably results in mis-hits.

The combination of good timing and rhythm I shall call "tempo." You must always hit with tempo to get the consistently best results with any club, regular iron as well as woodiron. Woodirons won't forgive poor tempo, although they will be more forgiving than regular irons. But to get the best results with woodirons, your swing with any given club must be in good tempo so that you impart the maximum amount of your natural hitting power without slipping over the edge into "forced" power.

Again, the beauty of woodirons is that once you get used to them and see what they can do, they almost forbid you from indulging in the urge to overhit them. They are the best natural inhibitors of forcing and overhitting and "swinging from the top" I know of. They truly do the work of achieving both the distance and the direction built into them—much more so than conventional irons. All you have to do is apply your natural physical power to them through the tempo that's unique to you. This does not mean the seemingly lazy swing of a Julius Boros or the fierce, lunging swing of an Arnold Palmer. It means a swing in which your club head strikes the ball without your body's excessively exerting itself, a swing whose tempo and force best suits you.

The bonus of having the woodirons accustom you to a good-tempo swing is, as I mentioned in the last chapter, that the same swing habits will spill over to your regular wood shots. Thus not only will you experience a radical improvement in that part of your game which normally calls for iron shots; your ordinary wood game will improve significantly as well.

At this time take a look at the *Woodiron Maximum Distance Chart* at the top of the next page.

The representative distances are based on personal data I have gathered from about forty golfers in each strength category. You will note that, starting with the 15 wood, each woodiron produces an additional eight yards in length, respectively, as the clubs descend in number through the 5 wood. We can say, then, that each yardage figure for a given woodiron is the length that is

WOODIRON MAXIMUM DISTANCE CHART

Wood Club	Iron Equiv.	Strong Male	Average Male	Strong Female/ Weak Male	Average Female
15 Wood	Sand wedge	125 yds.	105 yds.	90 yds.	70 yds.
14 Wood	10 Iron	133 yds.	113 yds.	98 yds.	78 yds.
13 Wood	9 Iron	141 yds.	121 yds.	106 yds.	86 yds.
12 Wood	8 Iron	149 yds.	129 yds.	114 yds.	94 yds.
11 Wood	7 Iron	157 yds.	137 yds.	122 yds.	102 yds.
10 Wood	6 Iron	165 yds.	145 yds.	130 yds.	110 yds.
9 Wood	5 Iron	173 yds.	153 yds.	138 yds.	118 yds.
8 Wood	4 Iron	181 yds.	161 yds.	146 yds.	126 yds.
7 Wood	3 Iron	189 yds.	169 yds.	154 yds.	134 yds.
6 Wood	2 Iron	197 yds.	177 yds.	162 yds.	142 yds.
5 Wood	1 Iron	205 yds.	185 yds.	170 yds.	150 yds.
4 Wood	—	220 yds.	195 yds.	180 yds.	160 yds.
3 Wood	—	235 yds.	205 yds.	190 yds.	170 yds.
Driver	—	250 yds.	225 yds.	200 yds.	180 yds.

built into that club, by virtue of its club-face loft, for each of the four strength categories.

The yardage figures assume, of course, a perfectly hit shot under neutral weather and golf-course conditions. Such factors as wind and uphill or downhill lies would alter these figures. I have presented the chart solely as a guide for you to determine what you can realistically expect in distance from each woodiron once you master it, depending on the general strength category you fall under. But you shouldn't expect the distances set out in the chart to be accurate to the yard when you start to use woodirons. As with conventional irons, the distance you get with any woodiron will vary with course conditions, with the circumstances of your swing, with your strength category, and with your ability to hit your shots fairly straight.

The ultimate determination of the consistent distance you can expect to achieve with any given woodiron will come after you have gotten the feel of the clubs through the program I outline for you in the chapters to come. Once you've become accustomed to the clubs, you will probably find that the distances set out in the chart are fairly close to the yardages you will get under neutral conditions.

What's important to remember now is that each woodiron has built into it an approximately 8-yard distance difference from the club immediately above and below it in number. This is important because, for a top-notch golfer who makes the transition from irons to woodirons, these narrow distance differentials will be significant to his game, just as they are with irons. A top-notch golfer will need a full set of woodirons because he is accustomed to stroking the ball with tight accuracy.

However, the scratch golfer, unless he suffers from a physical problem such as Billy Dear's, is not likely to need the help wood-irons provide. It is you, the average-to-poor golfer, whom these clubs will really help. Pinpoint accuracy is not at present an important consideration in your game: you're usually happy to put the ball within 15 or 20 yards of where you want it to go on anything beyond a short shot. Thus, at least at the beginning of your transition to woodirons, you don't need to worry about obtaining the whole array of such clubs right off the bat. If you follow the program I will be outlining ahead, you will need to acquire only three wood-irons during its beginning stages. Only after you have become comfortable with these and have seen your scores begin to drop—in no more than a week's time if you follow my schedule—will you want to expand your set to include most or all of the woodirons from the 6 wood to the 15 wood. *(See Figs. 7 and 8.)*

Of course, if you do eventually carry a full set of these clubs, it will be like carrying ten conventional irons. If you also play with a driver, two fairway woods such as a 3 wood and a 4 or 5 wood, and the requisite putter, you will have reached the legal limit of the clubs you can carry. If you want to pack a conventional wedge or some other iron among your clubs for emergency situations, you

Figure 7

Figure 8

will have to discard at least one of your woods. I would recommend removing the 4 wood.

So—you are now ready to begin your introduction to the Woodiron Method. Because the 15 wood is the key to the method, we will start with that club. The reasons for doing so are twofold. First, as I have said, it will provide the quickest and cheapest way for you to learn whether the Woodiron Method is for you. Second, although I have no doubt you'll fall in love with woodirons, in case you don't you will not have lost anything but the modest cost of a 15 wood and a few hours of introductory practice with it.

The seven-day program

To repeat, the 15 wood is the woodiron equivalent of the conventional sand wedge (see Fig. 9), but its utility on the golf course far exceeds that of the sand iron. It will become your most oft-used club after the putter.

Ordinary golfers use their sand irons, usually, only to get out of sand traps. Professionals and superior amateurs use the club much more frequently—for medium-length pitch shots to the green from rough, for lofted chip shots, and so on. What the 15 wood will provide you with is the ability to produce the kind and variety of shots that many pros execute with their sand irons. To the average golfer, the sand iron is a strictly limited club. In the hands of the top touring pro, it is a kind of "super" pitching wedge. And that's what a 15 wood is: a super pitching wedge that you can also use to great effect for getting out of all but perhaps the deepest bunkers. Indeed, because of the bulk of its club head, the 15 wood will be inherently more effective than the conventional sand wedge in getting you out of bunkers. (See Fig. 10.)

The 15 wood is your introduction to the Woodiron Method. The program of transition to woodirons that you are about to embark on covers a full week of daily practice and playing. The program assumes that you have a week's worth of free daily time in which to carry it out. Of course, many of you won't want to wait until you have a week of free time; you will want to start out anyway

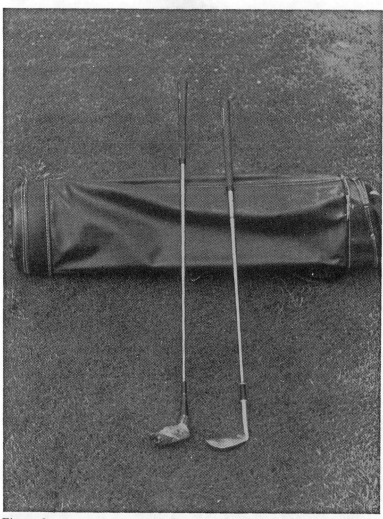

Figure 9

Figure 10

on the program. If this is the case with you, no problem. All you need to do is resolve to give up your next seven regular golfing days and devote them instead to learning the Woodiron Method according to the seven-day schedule set forth in these pages. Don't worry—whether you carry out the program in a single week or over the course of several weeks, you will not be giving up golf. You will be playing plenty of golf. At the beginning, however, it will be a little different from what you're used to.

This is all part of the learning experience. Yes, there are other ways to get into the Woodiron Method; you could even buy a whole set of woodirons and simply start playing with them. But my experience has shown that every method should have a method. The seven-day method of transition and learning I have worked out for this book has proven to be the best and most efficient way for golfers to make the complete transition to woodirons. Which is to say that the golfers whom I have seen benefit most from the switch to woodirons are those who have followed this seven-day, step-by-step program. Each day will include a morning session of practice and an afternoon session of actual playing.

In order to start the first day of the program, of course, you will need to acquire a 15 wood. They are not hard to find, but you may have to travel beyond your local pro shop or neighborhood retail sports store to purchase one. Most pro shops do not stock them; nor usually do small sporting-goods outlets, although they can often order them for you. To acquire a 15 wood immediately, you will probably have to go to a sporting-goods emporium located in or near a large city, or to a suburban shopping mall—a store that carries a wide range of golf equipment.

There are four golf-club companies that presently make high-numbered woods: Shakespeare, V.I.D., Wilson, and Northwestern. Any large store or chain operation will carry clubs by at least one of these manufacturers. High-numbered woods—woodirons—will range in price from about $20 for a cheaply made club to about $35 for a club of better quality. This is not a paid endorsement, but I have found that the woodirons made by Northwestern are the most widely available and are also of good quality. Northwestern makes them in both men's and women's sizes—the club heads are the same size for a particular wood but the men's shafts are an inch or so longer—and in right-handed and southpaw models. Northwestern's 15 wood sells for about $30, and their other woodirons are priced similarly.

You needn't worry about such exotic factors as swing weights and shaft flexes. All of the commercially marketed woodirons are made with single standard swing weights and flexes. It will only be later, once you've discovered the difference your commercial woodirons have made in your game, that you might want to have a set custom-made to your weight and flex specifications. Although I believe this would be a needless extra expense, there are at least half a dozen custom manufacturers around the country who will make woodirons to order. The cost averages about $100 per club. The best source for information about custom club makers is the pro shop at your golf course.

You have purchased a 15 wood (or perhaps borrowed one). Now what do you do? Get ready to begin the program that will turn your golf game into a much more satisfying and rewarding pastime than it is today.

The first day:
introduction to the
woodiron method

The first day of the transition program is designed to familiarize you with the feel, swing, and action of the 15 wood. For this you should take the club to the practice tee at your golf course, or to a public driving range. You will spend about two hours and exhaust several large buckets of balls on drills that will give you a good idea of the club's potential and put you in tune with it.

After you learn to hit comfortably and proficiently with the 15 wood, hitting all the other woodirons will become a cinch. So too will hitting your regular woods, for the woodirons will impress you by how easily they do the work. Once you experience this, to repeat again, you will no longer be tempted to slash away at the ball on your regular wood shots and drives.

At the practice range you will not start out by trying to hit full 15-wood shots. You will work up to these with a number of intermediate drills. But before you start the drills, you should know something about the grip, stance, address, and swing involved in the proper use of the 15 wood and the other wood irons.

Grip: There are many effective ways of gripping a golf club that fall within the parameters of the standard or ideal grip configuration. Every golfer's grip, though close to the standard, is unique to him or her. Some of you use the interlocking-finger grip. Some of you use the overlapping-finger grip. Some of you use a baseball-type grip. Some of you grip with your hands shaded slightly around to the left. Some grip dead center so that the V's of your thumbs point up to your right ear or shoulder. Some of you grip with your hands pronated farther to the right on the shaft.

Everyone's grip, then, is slightly different. When it comes to adapting yourself to the 15 wood or any other woodiron, you do not need to make any adjustments in the basic grip you have always used—assuming that your grip has served you reasonably well. However, if your basic grip is one that is designed to compensate for a tendency to hit extreme hooks or slices, you may find that when you start stroking the 15 wood you will no longer require it.

I am not talking about intentional draws or fades, for which expert golfers adjust their grips and stances to produce such shots. What I'm talking about is the annoying tendency to hook and slice naturally, which is usually the result of a defect in your swing. Rather than correct the swing, many golfers adjust their basic grips—going to "weak" or "strong" grips—to neutralize the defect in their swing that produces hooks and slices, shanks and slubs.

If you normally play with such a "crutch" grip, you will probably find it no longer necessary once you start using woodirons. This is because the woodirons have another marvelous quality, which is to send the ball flying straight in spite of the defect in one's swing that would normally send it offline with an iron. In this respect, then, you may have to readjust your normal strong or weak compensatory grip back to a more or less standard golf grip.

My natural golf swing has always had an outside-in defect that tended to produce moderate to severe slices whenever I succumbed to the impulse to overhit. This is probably the most common swing defect of all poor golfers. I tried to solve my problem by changing my grip to a "strong" grip—that is, gripping the club with my hands rotated around to the right and thereby closing the club face as it struck the ball. This worked to a degree in solving my slicing problem when I played with conventional clubs. But when I started to use woodirons with the same grip, my tendency was to pull and hook. So I went back to a normal grip and—*voilà!*—I began to hit my woodiron shots straight and true.

So, then, as you take in hand the 15 wood, and later the other woodirons, if your grip is a neutral one and you have no severe directional problems when you hit a golf ball with your driver, leave your grip as it is. If your basic grip is a "strong" or "weak" one, used to compensate for directional problems, be prepared to return to a neutral grip with the woodirons. (See Figs. 11, 12, and 13.)

Stance: Nor does playing with the 15 wood or any other woodiron require a significant change in the stance you would normally assume when playing a conventional wedge or other iron. What you have been comfortable with when using irons will serve you well as you change to woodirons. What you want to achieve on any golf shot is maximum effective swing arc between the horizontal and vertical. Some golfers stand too close to the ball and thereby produce a swing that is too close to vertical, restricting their body movement and depriving them of power. Others stand too far away, producing a swing that is too close to horizontal. They get power but lose directional control because of the lunging they have to do.

The proper golf swing depends primarily for its effectiveness on the player's standing at the proper distance from the ball. And here is where you will notice the sharp difference between irons and woodirons when you first address a ball with the latter. The shafts of woodirons are longer than those of their iron equivalents. Thus you cannot stand up to a ball with a 15 wood as you would with a wedge, with a 10 wood as you would with a 6 iron, and so on. Woodirons are, after all, wood clubs with iron loft angles. And they are made to be swung more like woods than irons.

So, as you play any woodiron, you can maintain your normal stance, but you should set up farther away from the ball as dictated by the club's longer shaft length. This means far enough away so that your swing won't be too upright, but not so far away that you have to lunge at the ball.

The best test of your stance with any woodiron is to compare it to your stance when hitting a regular wood. Remembering that a woodiron is a wood and not an iron, and that it requires what is

Figure 11

Figure 12

Figure 13

Figure 14

Figure 15

Figure 16

basically a wood swing, you will quickly learn how best to set yourself up with a woodiron, vis-à-vis your distance from the ball, to achieve the optimum swing arc. (See Figs. 14, 15, and 16.)

Address: If stance relates to your distance away from the ball, address refers to how you set your feet, body, hands, and club in forward or rearward opposition to the ball. And here is where a really significant difference comes into play between the conventional irons and the woodirons.

Standard golfing procedure when executing iron shots is to address the ball so that it is slightly to the rear of the center line of your body when playing the highest-number iron. As the number of the iron you use descends, you are supposed to address the ball proportionately forward of this point so that, by the time you get to the 2 iron, it is well in front of the center line of your body. (See Figs. 17 and 18.)

With woodirons you don't have to worry about adjusting the address relationship of your body to the ball with every shot. There will of course be times on the golf course when you will have to do so if you are confronted by extreme uphill or downhill lies, or by other

Figure 17   *Figure 18*

Figure 19   *Figure 20*

special-situation shots. But most of the time you will address the ball in the same way you do when you hit a regular wood—that is, with the ball opposite the inside of your left heel. (See Figs. 19 and 20.) This is because, again, you will be playing full woodiron shots, even the 15 wood, with your basic wood swing.

But what about backspin, you may ask? How do you get the kind of backspin that causes the ball to bite into and hold the green when you hit a good iron shot?

The answer is that even with the ball forward in your address, the woodiron club head will impart sufficient backspin to stop the ball within a few feet of its landing spot. The effect is enhanced by the height you will find yourself getting from your woodirons. Height and distance are the two basic ingredients of any good shot to the green that is on line—ingredients you have most likely seldom been able to achieve. With the woodirons, you will seldom fail to achieve them.

Swing: By the time you are ready to leave for the practice range, you will have already tried a few swings with your new 15 wood. If you have swung as you would with an iron, stop now so that you don't get off on the wrong foot. If you have swung as you would with a wood, sweeping through and just brushing the grass, also stop. The proper full swing for the 15 wood and the other woodirons is just like the woods, to be sure—especially in the take-away, backswing, downswing, impact, follow-through, and body action involved in all five phases. But there *is* a difference.

The difference occurs at the impact moment. Whereas with the driver and regular fairway woods your goal is to barely brush the ground as you sweep through the ball, with the woodirons you will want to make more contact with the ground. The higher the number of the wood, the more contact is desirable—to the point that with the higher-numbered woodirons you will even take shallow divots on full shots.

Divots, you say! Don't they demand an iron swing?

Not at all. If you inspect the metal soleplate of your 15 wood, you'll notice that it has a fairly sharp forward edge where it angles up to meet the scored hitting surface of the club face. (See Fig. 21.) In a graphic way this tells you the whole story of how and why the woodirons are such effective and easy clubs to play with. Your goal when swinging with a woodiron is to strike the ball square in the center of the club face, not lower on the club face as with ordinary woods. Ordinary woods have soleplates whose forward edges are beveled or rounded where they join the bottom of the club face. Moreover the soleplate does not project upward to infringe on the club face itself.

With an ordinary wood, then, your object is to hit the ball at the bottom center of the club face, with the dull-edged soleplate just brushing the ground. With a full-swing woodiron you don't want to strike the ball with the bottom center of the club face because, if you do, the upward-projecting piece of the soleplate will make contact with the ball and you will lose much of the backspin factor provided by the scored grooves on the club face. Also you will hit too high up on the ball to achieve the loft provided by the angle of the club face, not to mention that you will probably cut the ball's cover with the soleplate's sharp edge. (See Fig. 22.)

When you strike the ball with a woodiron properly, you want to hit it so that the ball meets the club face at its center, above the

Figure 21

Figure 22

sharp-edged, projecting soleplate. Thus the edge of the soleplate must make contact with the ground. If you are hitting from a fairway lie in which the ball is sitting up nicely on a half-inch cushion of grass, you will not need to take a divot. But your ball is just as likely to be resting snug to the ground on one of those well-watered, tightly mowed fairway carpets that are so common on better golf courses these days. To hit it properly, you must allow the leading edge of the soleplate to slice through the soft turf. This is why the leading edge is so sharp—to assist in the process and to allow you to take a divot without jarring or bouncing the club, as would happen if you made such solid contact with the ground with a regular fairway wood.

The same principle operates when you play woodiron shots from the rough. At times you will play from a lie in which your ball is sitting on a cushion of rough grass. Here you do not want to take a divot because by doing so you would strike the ball too high up on the club face. On the other hand, if your ball is deep down in the rough, close to or on the ground, a proper hit will produce a divot.

The idea of the woodiron divot, then, is to strike the ball with a normal wood swing and let the sharp leading edge of the club face make the divot on its own. The sharp edge, by slicing through the turf, or by efficiently slicing through the high grass on a shot from the rough, is what enables the woodiron's club head to play through the ball without being impeded by ground or grass.

Now you are probably ready to ask: How do I get a divot when I'm using a wood swing instead of an iron swing? The answer is by *staying down* on the ball, just as you're supposed to do when hitting a fairway wood or driver.

One of the commonest misconceptions about the standard wood swing is that the golfer is supposed to scoop the ball into the air with the swing itself. This is a real bugaboo among golfers who do not hit conventional woods well. Their problem is that their concept of the swing is all wrong. By thinking in these terms, they try to scoop the ball off the grass physically with their swings. The results are frequently topped shots or low short skimmers, caused by their sudden lifting action as club head meets ball. This is called not letting the club do its work.

The correct wood swing is executed by arcing the club head

simultaneously *down* and *through* the ball. At the moment of impact the arc of the club head should not be in the slightest upward, but should be traveling still slightly downward. Only in this way can proper contact be made and the club face allowed to do the work its loft angle is designed to do, i.e., propel the ball forward and into the air. When the wood swing is executed correctly, the club head does not begin its upward arc until a millisecond after the ball has been struck.

On shots with drivers off tees this is not likely to be noticed, since the artificial elevation of the ball leaves enough space between it and the ground so that the bottom of the club head does not touch the ground. But it is readily noticeable on a correctly executed fairway-wood shot. When you hit with a 2, 3, 4, or 5 wood and you make the shot with the correct swing, the bottom of the club head will brush or even bounce off the ground a few centimeters ahead of where the ball lay. This is because the club-head arc is still slightly downward at the moment of impact. It is only upon its contact with the ground that the arc begins to ascend. By this time the ball has already been launched from the club face and into the air.

The basic woodiron swing is identical, then, to the standard correct long-wood swing. The only difference in club-head effect is that instead of brushing or bouncing lightly off the ground a few centimeters in front of the ball, the woodiron will actually slice through the turf a few centimeters ahead of the ball, creating a shallow divot—particularly when the ball lies tight to the ground. A slight divot in a tight lie is the best immediate evidence you have that you've struck the ball correctly on a full-swing woodiron shot. (See Fig. 23.)

How can you ensure getting this effect? By "staying down" on the ball as you swing through, just as you're supposed to do when you swing a regular wood club. By permitting the club to do the work rather than trying to do it yourself. The only work you have to do is to get the club head to the ball and make sure that its arc hasn't started upward before it strikes the ball.

Staying down on the ball does not mean "getting under" it. Many poor players, in their desire to do away with topped wood shots, tend to overcompensate by lunging down at the ball with

Figure 23

their club heads, especially on drives. Usually the result is another kind of mis-hit, this one a pop fly caused by the club head's jamming into the ground just behind the ball.

As you begin to take a few full practice swings with your new 15 wood, keep all these factors relaxedly in mind. You don't need to make any significant adjustments in your normal grip, stance, or address except to make sure, using your normal stance and mode of address, that you set up far enough away from the ball, and that you position yourself so that the ball is well forward of the midline of your body but inside a line opposite your left heel. As for the swing, this is the easy part. If you have a proficient wood swing already, all you have to do is apply it to the woodirons.

For those of you whose regular wood swings are not so proficient, learning how to swing the woodiron clubs properly will be a boon. The woodiron swing is nothing more than a controlled, "swing-within-yourself" wood swing. Once you grow accustomed to it and discover how your shots fly far, straight, and true, you will very quickly adjust your faulty regular wood swing to match it. Suddenly your regular wood game will improve too.

What makes this a certainty? Well, take another close look at the club head of the 15 wood, then grip the shaft and waggle it about for a few seconds, getting the feel of its heft and balance. You will notice that the 15 wood feels considerably heavier at the club head than a wedge. The same is true with the other woodirons: the club heads not only have significantly more physical bulk, but they're heavier than their iron equivalents at the striking point. It is in these two qualities that the woodirons are much more effective at doing the work than conventional irons. You will rapidly learn that when you hit a ball with a woodiron, there is absolutely no need to force the shot or try to put extra "oomph" into it. The club head's weight and mass, plus the club-face angle, are extremely efficient at combining to get the ball up and away with the application of normal swing force. All you have to do as you swing is make sure that grip, stance, and swing are in alignment so that the ball goes relatively straight. When you begin to realize how easy it is to hit woodiron shots in prescribed distances, heights, and directions, and how easy it is to hit them consistently, you will apply those same principles to your ordinary wood—tee and fairway—shots.

I call this "taming" the long woods. Take an average, wide-open, 400-yard-long par-4 hole, for instance. Everyone's impulse is to hit the longest drive possible so as to reduce the length of the second shot to the green. So they flail away at the tee shot, hoping for more distance than they are naturally capable of. Instead, by forcing the drive, more often than not they hit the ball way offline, leaving themselves with a second shot that is not only more difficult but nowhere close to the 150 yards in length they had hoped for.

After they become woodiron players, though, they will realize that they don't always need to get as close to the green as possible on their drive. A 220-yard straight drive will leave them 180 yards from the pin and facing a second shot that can be much more easily executed with a 7 or 8 wood than a 3 or 4 iron. Since they will no longer possess a fear of hitting low-iron approach shots, they won't be overcome by the urge to hit their drive 250 yards. They will be content with a 220-yard tee shot that gives them a clear 180-yard approach with a 7 or 8 wood.

With all this firmly in mind, you are now ready to go to the practice range and begin your week-long transition to woodirons. Take only your new 15 wood and leave the rest of your clubs behind. Except for your putter, you will not be using any of them for the next few days.

The first day: morning session

Now you are at the practice range with your new 15 wood and several buckets of balls at the ready. As I cautioned earlier you do not start out by trying to hit full-swing shots with the 15 wood. You should work up to those by engaging in the following series of drills.

FIRST DRILL

Line up 20 golf balls about a foot apart. (If you are at a public driving range that provides only stalls from which to practice, you will have to put down a new ball for each shot. Do not do these drills from tees on the rubber mats; use the simulated grass mats.) Then set up a target (a hat or an empty bucket) 10 yards in front of you. Grip the 15 wood in an extremely "full-choke" position. But instead of wrapping the forefinger of your lower hand around the shaft as you would normally, extend it down the side of the shaft so that it acts as a lever. (See Fig. 24.) Take a few wristy "putting-stroke"-type practice swings with your extended forefinger pressed against the shaft and your feet close together. (See Figs. 25 and 26.)

This will be your basic short-chipping swing with the 15 wood. Keep practicing, letting the bottom of the club brush the ground

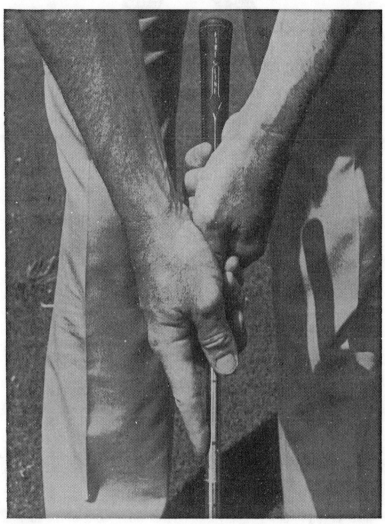

Figure 24

Figure 25   *Figure 26*

and then following through, mostly with your wrists, until you get the feel of it. Then step up to the first in your row of 20 balls.

What you are going to do initially is aim for the target 10 yards away and try to chip each ball so that it hits the hat or bucket on the fly. You will be using the 15 wood just as you would a very soft wedge. But instead of jamming the club head into the ball without a follow-through, you *will* follow through much as you would if you were putting.

The first few balls you hit undoubtedly will skid well beyond or dribble well short of your target. But they will go straight. After five or six you will have a clear visual and tactile image of how effective the 15 wood is in getting the ball into the air with a minimum of effort on your part. (See Figs. 27, 28, 29, and 30.)

Continue the drill through the remainder of the row of balls, letting the club head do all the work and exerting no more force

Figure 27

Figure 28

Figure 29

Figure 30

than you would if you were stroking 10-yard putts. Then put down another row of 20 balls. This time, instead of trying to hit your target on the fly, adjust the force and tempo of the swing so as to bounce each ball in front of the target and make it roll as close as possible.

Congratulations—you have learned the basics of how to stroke short easy chip shots with the 15 wood. Now put down another row of 20 balls. This time really concentrate on chip-rolling the balls to the target, deliberating over each shot and getting each ball as close as you can. On this round of shots you will finally begin to get a real feel of the 15 wood as an all-purpose around-the-green club. You will, at the same time, be impressed by the manner in which it does the work.

If you have any doubts, borrow a pitching wedge or some other iron you are accustomed to utilizing on short chips. Stroke 20 balls with this to the target. Then go back and stroke another 20 with the 15 wood. See the difference?

SECOND DRILL

You are now ready to proceed to a longer category of chip shots. This time move your target to a distance of 30 yards and drop another 20 balls in a row, a foot apart. Choke-grip the 15 wood again, as you did for the first drill. But instead of extending your forefinger down the shaft, this time wrap it around in your normal grip configuration. (See Fig. 31.)

Using a more widespread stance this time, begin to stroke each of the balls at the target, aiming to hit the target on the fly. As you go through your first 20 balls, you'll find that you need to exert *too much* force to reach the target with your hands on the grip in the extreme choked position. You are doing the work that the club head is designed to do.

Put down another 20 balls. This time, move your hands up the grip to a half-choke position, still with your fingers wrapped around in your normal grip configuration. (See Fig. 32.) Hit the next 20 balls like this, adjusting the pendulum length and force of your swing, as well as your foot spread, until you are able to loft the ball consistently near the target. With each straight hit, the ball

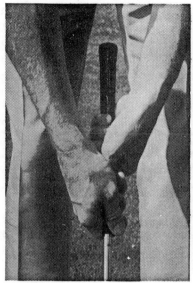
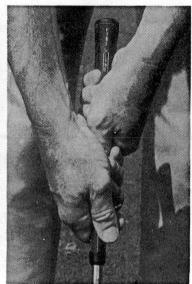

Figure 31   *Figure 32*

should describe a parabola that reaches about 10 feet in height, then descends within a few yards of the target. You may need to hit another 20 or so balls to achieve this consistently, but once you do you are ready to go on to the next step in the drill.

This time, using the same half-choke grip, try to stroke the next 20 balls so that each ball falls short of the target and rolls to or past it. To do this, you will reduce the force, but not the arc, of your swing, which by now you can identify as a quarter swing. (See Figs. 33, 34, 35, and 36.) Hit still another 40 balls, adjusting your swing force as you go until you can consistently loft the ball and roll it close to the target—say to within 5 yards.

You have now gotten a good idea of how to hit a medium chip shot with the 15 wood. (We will get to the nuances of chipping at a later session.) It is now time to familiarize yourself with the long chip. By "long chip" I do not mean a running chip—a ball hit low to bounce and roll a long distance to a target; this too we will get into later. I mean a lofted shot designed to land within a few yards of the target with a minimum of roll.

Figure 33

Figure 34

Figure 35

Figure 36

THIRD DRILL

To learn this shot with the 15 wood, extend your target out to a distance of 60 yards. Still employing your half-choke grip, this time hit 20 balls with a fuller swing. As you go through the first 20 balls, adjust your swing—keeping its force constant—until you arrive at the swing arc and force you find most effective for the shot. For some of you it may be a half swing (see Fig. 37), for others a three-quarter swing (see Fig. 38), for others somewhere in between and for a few somewhat more than a three-quarter swing. The important thing to concentrate on is finding the correct constant swing arc and swing force that get the ball to the target most consistently without your having to exert excessive force.

What you are trying to do is find the smoothest, most "tempo"-ized swing you can to produce the desired result for this 60-yard lofted shot with a half-choke grip. This is your basic long chip shot, but for learning purposes it's more than that. Why? Because the tempo and force you settle on as being best for you in executing this shot will become the swing reference for all your other, fuller, woodiron swings.

Figure 37   *Figure 38*

In other words, the rhythm-and-execution factor you find most effective for the long lofted chip will be the rhythm-and-execution factor you will want to put into all your 15-wood shots and all your shots with the other woodirons. It is the achievement of this constant swing factor that you will concentrate on in your future woodiron drills. Once it becomes set in your mind and body in the form of "muscle memory," you will have overcome the most difficult obstacle in making the transition from irons to woodirons. You will have settled upon the precise optimum distance and height you can consistently get with each club on a full-swing shot, and you will have to worry thereafter only about precise direction.

So work at this drill through another 30 or 40 balls, or until you can stroke each ball on the fly to within a few yards of your target 60 yards away.

Next, using the same swing tempo, but reducing your swing arc by a fraction, hit another 30 or 40 balls so that, achieving about 30 feet of loft, they land 10 yards in front of the target and bounce toward it.

Now you will have a good beginner's feel both for the long chip shot (or short pitch) and for the proper swing tempo of the woodirons in general. Remember, the swing tempo you want is that which lets the angle, bulk, and weight of the club head do most of the work. All you have to do is impart and maintain control over the swing and its arc so that the woodiron's "work factors" can come fully into play.

FOURTH DRILL

This is what I call the full-swing, half-choke drill. Again, put down 20 balls but get rid of your target; at the beginning you don't want to aim at anything. Instead, you want to find out how far you can stroke the ball with the 15 wood, using a half-choke grip but a full swing within the tempo and force limits you established in the previous drill.

Stroke each ball with what would be a full swing, if you were using a wedge or other high iron. (See Figs. 39 and 40.) This is the swing you will use on lofted medium-pitch shots to a green—generally from 50 to 100 yards out if you are a golfer of average

Figure 39   *Figure 40*

power. As you full-swing-hit each ball, concentrate solely on two things: (1) the tempo you have established for shorter swings, and (2) staying down on the ball.

As you go through the first 20 balls, you will probably find that you get good distance and direction but not enough loft. This is okay when you play long pitch and run shots to greens that are unguarded in front by bunkers or ponds. But what about when you need to clear such hazards and land on greens without much roll? For this you need backspin and loft—at least 60 feet at the top of the ball's parabola. To achieve this you will have to start doing something slightly different than you've done so far. And that is: start taking slight divots.

You'll recall that in the last chapter I said that, in order to get the optimum backspin and loft with a woodiron, you have to swing so that the upward-projecting edge of the club's metal soleplate is beneath the ball upon impact, and that the ball is struck only by the grooved surface of the wooden or plastic insert of the club face. And that to achieve this effect, you have to take a slight to moderate divot with the sharp leading edge of the soleplate. A divot ensures that you have gotten the soleplate sufficiently under the ball so that only the grooved face impacts with it.

To do this, you should not try to force a divot by jamming the club head into the ground. You simply stay down on your swing so that the club face strikes the ball a fraction of an inch lower, but strikes it before the club contacts the ground. (See Figs. 22 and 23.)

This, then, is what you will practice next.

FIFTH DRILL

This drill is the same as the fourth, but now you should try to take a slight divot with each full swing, half-choke shot. Put down 20 balls and forget about shooting to a target or achieving a particular distance. All you want to do here is maintain your tempo as you execute a full swing, and practice slicing a shallow divot out of the turf in conjunction with striking the ball. The ideal divot should be no more than 1/4 inch deep and 3 inches in length. (See Fig. 23.) Anything deeper or longer means that you are getting too far under the ball, or else are jamming the club head into the ball like an iron. In either case you will lose distance as well as direction, since the resistance of the turf will twist the club face and abruptly slow down club-head speed as it moves through the ball. You will know if you are taking too deep a divot when you feel the ground's resistance and there is a tendency not to be able to follow through on your swing easily. (All woodiron shots, except for short chips, should always be completed with full follow-throughs.)

When you hit your first 20 balls of the drill, you will make mistakes on most of them as you try to achieve the correct divots and follow-throughs. You will hit in front of the ball, you will hit on top of the ball, and so on. That's okay; let the first 20 balls teach you what you shouldn't do. Then put down another 20 and try again.

This time, you'll begin to get the hang of the full-swing, half-

choke divot pitch shot. And as you get the hang of it, your balls will
fly higher and stop with less roll.

Once you can get 80 to 100 feet in height with regularity (it
may take hitting several more groups of balls), it is time to start
targeting your shots for distance and direction.

SIXTH DRILL

Pace off the distance between where you've been hitting and the
general area in which most of your balls have landed. Then set up a
target in the middle of that area and go back to the practice tee.
The distance may be anywhere from 50 to 110 yards, depending on
your natural power and your tempo with the half-choke, full-swing
divot pitch shot. Whatever the distance, that is the correct yardage
for you on this shot (at least for now; as you become more expert
with the 15 wood, you will eventually be able to increase or lessen
your distances at will by modulating your swing arc and grip length.

Now hit another 20 divot shots while aiming for the target
you've set out. The first 20 shots will probably be a disappointment.
But don't get discouraged—now that you're aiming, you are no
doubt subconsciously trying to manipulate the balls with your
hands and arms. Go back to the basics—full swing, tempo, stay
down, divot, follow-through—and hit another 20 shots. There, you
see? It makes a difference, doesn't it? Out of the second 20 balls,
you managed to stroke 4 or 5 that had all the look, feel, and touch of
professional pitch shots.

Hit another 20, and still more after that, until at least 15 out
of every 20 loft high and true and drop close to your target. By that
time your swing will feel comfortable and you'll feel confident that
you are capable of doing whatever you have to do with the 15 wood
to execute the shot consistently.

SEVENTH DRILL

Now you are ready to advance to the all-out full-swing, full-grip 15
wood pitch-approach shot. To begin, move your grip up to the end

of the shaft. Review what I said in the last chapter about grip, stance, address, and swing. Then put down a row of 20 balls and ignore the target you set out for the last drill.

The point of this drill is to establish the maximum distance you are capable of getting with the 15 wood, while also getting maximum loft. This does not mean you should attack the first 20 balls with all your might. On the contrary, hit them with the tempo you have established previously. Don't worry about making divots on the first round; simply make good contact with the ball and execute a smooth, high follow-through. (See Fig. 41.)

You will probably mis-hit a few of the first 20 balls as you adjust to the proper stance, address, and swing tempo. Hit another 20, this time trying to groove your swing. Now hit 20 more. By this time you'll be making good contact with almost every shot and will be playing each one high and for good distance.

Figure 41

EIGHTH DRILL

After you've completed the final part of the previous drill, pace off the distance to where most of your last 20 balls landed. It might be anywhere from 60 to 130 yards, depending on your natural power, on whether you are a man or woman, on the arc and force of your swing, and so on. The distance you arrive at we will call your beginning "maximum distance factor" with the 15 wood stroked fully and without a divot.

Let's say the distance you have paced off is an even 100 yards. Set up your target at this spot, go back to the practice tee, and hit another full-swing 20 shots aimed at it, without taking divots. You will find that as you become more accustomed to the shot, your balls gradually will carry past your target—perhaps 10 to 20 yards farther.

Pace off the distance of the longest ball you've hit. This now becomes your intermediate "maximum distance factor" with the 15-wood—that is, the maximum distance you can hit with the club, using comfortable force and tempo at this intermediate stage of learning, and without taking a divot. This is a shot you will use often, especially when approaching open-fronted greens. Although it is a high pitch shot from a good distance—whatever your maximum distance factor turns out to be—you will get some bounce-and-roll with it because you won't take a divot. Thus you can use it to great effect, when hitting pitch shots to open-fronted greens, by landing the ball short of the green and bouncing it on.

Let's say the maximum distance you have measured after this drill is 120 yards. Move your target out to that distance and go back to the practice tee for the next drill.

NINTH DRILL

Put down another 20 balls and hit them—full-grip, full-swing—toward the target. As your swing becomes more grooved and controlled, the distance you consistently get with each nondivot shot may stay about the same or increase by another 10 to 15 yards. If your target is now at 120 yards and you begin to stretch out your shots to 130 yards, without overswinging, this will become your final "maximum distance factor" with the 15 wood. In other words, this is the distance you can confortably and consistently carve out by letting the club do most of the work and by not forcing the shot or overswinging at the ball. Everything you do from here on in with the 15 wood, and the rest of the woodirons, will be based on this distance factor.

Whether the maximum distance factor you have arrived at with the 15 wood is 130 yards, 50 yards, or any yardage in between, you can expect to be able to add to it 6 to 10 yards, or an average of 8 yards, with each consecutively lower numbered woodiron. If your maximum distance factor in the air with the 15 wood is 110 yards, say, a 14 wood will get you about 118 yards on the fly, a 13 wood 126 yards, and so on. Once you have worked out your 15-wood distance factor, refer once again to the distance chart on page 30. By establishing your own 15-wood distance factor, you can now create a distance chart tailored to yourself. Work out a personalized chart on paper, adding eight yards to your 15-wood distance factor for each lower-numbered woodiron, and keep it handy. This chart will become your beginning distance guide for all your woodirons. I say "beginning" because, as you become more proficient with the 15 wood and the other woodirons, you will probably find your average distance factors for each club lengthening. Thus you will need to revise your personal chart upward until the ultimate figure for each woodiron becomes well fixed in your mind.

Now, hit another 40 balls—full-swing, no-divot—with your 15 wood. Aim each shot at your target and observe how far past the target each lands on the fly. Average out the additional distance in your head. This will confirm your maximum 15-wood distance factor for now.

TENTH DRILL

This is your next to last drill from the practice tee this morning. You have established your 15-wood's maximum distance factor, using a full controlled swing and without taking a divot. But many of your full-swing distance shots with this club, just as with a conventional wedge, will be shots that you need to stop in a fairly short distance once the ball lands—shots, for instance, over sand or

water to small greens from some distance away. For these, you will
want to make full-swing divot shots. Taking a divot will reduce your
distance factor by 5, 10, maybe even 15 yards. If you are faced with
such a shot from a distance that is equivalent to the maximum
distance factor of your 15 wood, you will probably fall short of your
target if you execute a divot shot with that club. You will carry the
shot off in much better style by using your 14 or 13 wood. The point
of this drill then, is to accustom you to full-swing divot shots, and at
the same time to determine your distance factor with such shots
when using the 15 wood.

Leave your target where it was earlier, which is now 10 to 20
yards short of your maximum 15-wood distance factor. Put down
another 20 balls in a row. Aiming at the target, begin to hit full-
swing shots at it. But this time try to take the same kinds of divots
you learned with the half-choke full-swing shot of the fifth drill.
Don't press, don't force, don't try to use the club like an iron. Ease
into the divot shots, making sure to keep the proper arc, tempo,
and follow-through with your full swing.

Your first 20 shots will feel a little awkward after you have
just hit 40 or 50 full-swing nondivot shots. So put down another 20
balls and go at it again, and another 20 after that. Judge your
effectiveness by the manner in which each ball soars toward and
lands near the target. You will begin to see the balls land with very
little bounce and roll. This is due to the backspin you impart to
them by taking divots. At first your divots will be too shallow or
deep, but as you progress through still another 20 balls you will
begin to master the shot.

Now pace off the on-the-fly distances of your last 20 shots
and average them. The average will be shorter than your final
maximum distance factor, maybe even shorter than the yardage to
the target—which, you'll remember, was your beginning distance
factor with the full-swing 15-wood in the eighth drill. Whatever
your divot-shot average is, this for now will become your distance
factor on this full-swing 15-wood shot. As you become more
accustomed to it, your average will undoubtedly stretch. And you
will base your distance factor for similar divot shots with the lower-
numbered woodirons on it, using the same 8-yard differential.
Generally speaking, a divot shot with any woodiron should net you

10 to 15 yards less than you get with a "clean," or nondivot, shot. This rule operates whether you take a full-swing shot of either type, a three-quarter-swing shot, a half-swing shot, or whatever.

Wind up this drill by hitting another 40 balls with the divot shot only, concentrating now on consistency of direction, loft, and distance.

ELEVENTH DRILL

Now to the final drill of your first session with the 15 wood. Place two targets out on the practice fairway—one at a yardage equivalent to your maximum clean-shot distance factor with the club, the other at the shorter yardage equivalent to your average divot-shot distance factor.

Put down 20 balls, and this time alternate shots. Hit a full-swing clean shot with the first ball, aiming for the farther target. Then hit a full-swing divot shot with the second ball, shooting for the nearer target. Then another clean shot. Then a divot shot. And so on.

Here you are learning how to mix up the two basic full-swing 15-wood shots—a habit that will stand you in good stead as you take up the lower-numbered woodirons in the sessions to come. You will probably find on your first 20 balls that adjusting between clean and divot shots is at first awkward, If so, hit another 20 balls, and 20 after that, until hitting the two shots on an alternating basis feels natural. Concentrate at all times on good swing mechanics and on aiming at your respective targets. By the time you've finished, you will have a beginning mastery of the two basic shots. Moreover, you will have vivid visual and physical evidence of how much easier a 15 wood is to use than the highest-numbered irons for those crucial approach-to-the-green shots that are the do-or-die moments in the game of the average golfer.

The first day:
afternoon session

Now you are going to learn on the golf course itself, rather than at the practice range, how effective the 15 wood can be. If your course has a practice green with an abundant and fairly level approach fairway, some rough, and a few sand traps, by all means use it for this session. If not, you will have to select a regular hole out on the course to conduct this session. In the event of that, try to start your first day of woodiron work on a day when there aren't a lot of golfers playing the course. You don't want your concentration interrupted every few minutes by a twosome or foursome playing through the hole you have chosen to practice on.

Also, since many golf clubs would object strenuously to a member hitting a number of practice shots from the middle of a fairway and digging up a lot of turf, you can usually find a spot in the low rough, where the grass is fairly good and the greenskeeper will not mind your digging out a few divots. I suggest you move around as you practice, so that you do not damage any one area too much. You may find it necessary to change greens from time to time, depending upon play and the effects of your practice. For the purpose of this book and the instructions that follow, I will assume that you are lucky and your course has a practice fairway and green.

The morning session will have left you a bit tired, so give

yourself several hours to recover with a nice hot shower, a good lunch, even a nap. Then take your 15 wood out to the hole you have chosen to practice on with a large bag of balls.

FIRST DRILL

Pace off and set yourself up at a distance of 150 yards from the center of your practice green. Take plenty of easy full-swing warm-ups with your 15 wood, getting all the kinks out of your body from the morning session. Once you are warm and loose, drop 20 balls on the grass.

No one I know can hit a 15 wood 150 yards on the fly, so this is not what you are going to try to do in this first drill. What you are going to do is hit 20 clean, full-swing, 15-wood shots toward the green in order to see how close you can get to it. You may end up anywhere from 20 to 70 yards short, but that's fine. Concentrate on smooth swing tempo and force, and on hitting clean, straight, generously lofted shots—just the way you did this morning from the practice tee.

This drill will give you a good idea of what the 15 wood is capable of on the golf course, as well as the other woodirons you'll be getting into later. The most important thing you will note, if you are an average mid-to-high-handicap golfer, is that you consistently produce much better shots than you would if you were using a high-numbered iron. They go farther, higher, and straighter—all at once—than a comparable number of iron shots you might hit from the same spot. No, they may not reach the green, but that's not the point of this drill. The point is to get a better feel for your 15-wood maximum distance factor on the golf course as opposed to on the practice range, and also to etch in your mind's eye the kind of professional loft and carry the 15 wood can produce as you hit toward a green.

SECOND DRILL

Calculate the average distance *short* of the green your first 20 balls have come to rest. Then move closer to the green by that distance. Drop and hit another 20 full-swing nondivot 15-wood shots at the green. Assuming that the front of the green is open and you can bounce most of your shots onto it, you have almost found the correct distance factor for your long full-swing 15-wood pitch-approach shots. Assuming also that the pin is set in the center of the green but your shots are not getting within easy two-putt range of it—that is, you are leaving your balls well short of or well beyond the pin—adjust your distance accordingly and hit another 20 shots.

You will realize that a lot of what you are doing now—as compared to what you did on the practice range this morning—has as much to do with your psychology as it does with the physical mechanics of hitting the golf ball. Many golfers who can hit well off a practice tee get thoroughly "psyched out" by the golf course. They go from being relaxed to being constricted and tense at the sight of narrow fairways, hazards, and distant greens. These are the golfers who lose confidence in their clubs and tend to force their shots. They succeed most of the time only in buying trouble.

So, in addition to everything else you are going to be working on in these golf-course drills, you must concentrate on staying relaxed. Not lazy, but relaxed. You are not shooting for a score now, you are merely testing the 15 wood in various golf-course situations. There is no reason to force your shots; there is every reason to let the club show you the work it can do and the results it can produce.

Hit your next 20 shots with all this firmly in mind, then, and all the subsequent shots you'll be practicing in the drills ahead. If you do, you'll encounter few problems of tension and anxiety once you begin to play competitive golf with the woodirons a week from now. You will have learned good golf-course habits, which is nothing more than trusting your clubs to do the job.

Your next 20 shots to the open-fronted green, be they from 50 yards or 130 yards out or some distance between, should bring you consistently closer to the pin and give you a feeling of expanding satisfaction. Don't be afraid to enjoy it. Could you have placed the ball on the green as regularly with your usual pitching wedge or 9 iron? I doubt it.

THIRD DRILL

Now it's time to move closer to the green and start practicing high, full-swing divot shots designed to land on the putting surface and stop within a few yards. Don't aim for the flagstick particularly, just the middle of the green. As you go through your next 20 balls you will probably find, as you did this morning, that the transition to divot shots takes a little while to make successfully. Use your first 20 balls to make the transition, adjusting your yardage slightly from the green with each stroke until you have found your most consistent distance.

When you've found the right distance, hit another 20 divot shots—this time aiming for the flagstick. As you go through this round of 20, you will find yourself adjusting the force of your full swing until you've achieved a good feel of exactly what it takes in force and tempo to achieve the best shot time after time.

Now hit still another 20 balls, all the while trying to groove the force and tempo of your swing for the best results. It will take a while longer before the right swing with the right woodiron for the right distance on any pitch-to-the-green shot becomes second nature to you. But you are well on the way, and with this round of 20 shots you'll be amazed by how close you can get to the pin with beautifully lofted, back-spinning divot-pitch shots with the 15 wood.

Note: If you find yourself, in any of these first three drills, pulling or pushing most of your shots, or hooking or slicing, pause to realign your grip, stance, and address in accordance with the principles I outlined in Chapter 5. The most common cause of such defects in the flight of the ball is the tendency to swing too hard with too strong or weak a grip, or to otherwise force the shot. Make the right corrections before proceeding further.

FOURTH DRILL

By this time you have gotten the feel of both full-swing clean and full-swing divot-pitch shots from your maximum distances with the 15 wood. You are ready to proceed now to three-quarter and half-swing shots with a full grip, and similar shots with a half-choke grip, from various distances. These are medium-to-short pitch-to-the-green shots, each demanding loft, precise distance, stopping power, and a divot technique. You worked on these shots from the practice tee this morning. Now is the time to see them in action under the more realistic surroundings on the golf course.

Start with the three-quarter-swing full-grip shot by moving 10 yards closer to the green than you were when executing your full-swing divot shots in the last drill. Employing all the swing principles you used before, including a full follow-through, hit 20 balls at the pin with a three-quarter swing, taking a divot with each shot.

Once you determine your best distance factor for this shot, move another 10 or 15 yards closer in and stroke 20 more balls with a full-grip half swing. Keep it up with additional balls until you are able to hit the green and stop the ball within two-putt distance of the pin on at least half your shots.

Let's say you've determined that your maximum distance factor with the 15 wood is 120 yards and your full-swing divot-shot distance is 105 yards. Your three-quarter-swing divot-shot factor should then be about 90 yards and your half-swing factor about 80. It will be in this manner that you will keep adjusting your swing arc and grip length as your pitch shots shorten in length. (These distance-factor figures should be modified, of course, in accord with your actual distance factors.)

FIFTH DRILL

At less than a half-swing, full-grip divot-shot distance factor of 80 yards (or whatever your distance factor actually is), you will be dealing with shorter pitch-to-the-green divot shots. And with these you will go to full swings, three-quarter swings and half swings with a half-choke grip.

You have already learned the fundamentals of these pitch shots as a result of the morning session. Now you are going to practice actually hitting to a green with them. Start with the full-swing half-choke divot shot by moving 10 yards closer to the green than you were at the end of the last drill. Execute a few shots for distance, then adjust your distance as required. Now run through 40 balls with this shot, taking a divot each time and, as before, trying to get as close to the pin as possible.

When you have gotten comfortable with the shot and can put a goodly number of balls within realistic two-putt range, move in another 10 yards or so and repeat the drill with a half-choke three-quarter swing.

Repeat again, 10 or 15 yards closer in this time, with a half-choke half-swing divot shot, once more adjusting your distance until you find the one that's most consistent.

By the time you've completed this drill, you will have come to the low end—distance-wise—of the pitch-shot spectrum. That is, whether your distance factor with the last series is 60 yards or 30 yards, that distance is the shortest you can safely execute a lofted pitch shot, whether with 15 woodiron or a standard iron. Anything shorter becomes a chip shot—long, medium, or short, high or low—and demands a slightly different technique.

With the 15 wood, the only technical change you will need to make when stroking a low, or running, chip of 20 to 40 yards is that you won't take a divot. Instead, you will adjust the arc and force of your swing to the shot's distance and let the club face propel the ball up, forward, and straight, using a half-choke grip to execute the shot.

This is the best kind of chip to use when you've got an open-fronted green ahead of you. But often you will have to make a medium-to-long chip over some kind of hazard to get on the putting surface close to the hole. This means more loft and less roll, so that the ball stops quickly once it lands on the green.

As with any conventional iron used for such chip shots, this requires a further modification in technique with the 15 wood. The modification is the so-called cut shot, which is designed to achieve high loft over a relatively short distance. This shot, and the technique involved, takes perhaps a little more time to master than the other 15 wood shots. But once mastered, it will become both an easy shot to play and the shot that you will probably most often find yourself using with the club. Why? Because it's not just effective for chips *over* trouble; it's an almost foolproof maneuver for successfully shooting *out of* trouble onto the green. Before we take up the cut shot, though, we need to practice another chip shot.

SIXTH DRILL

This drill is to teach you the technique and feel of the long-to-medium running chip to an open green. Drop 20 balls 50 yards from the green if you are a strong hitter, 40 yards if you are an average hitter, 30 yards if you are a weak hitter. Address the first ball as you did in the last drill, that is, with a half-choke grip. But this time set up with your feet markedly closer together. (See Fig. 42.)

Now, executing a smooth half-swing, strike the ball toward the green by swinging firmly through it, taking no divot. The ball should fly forward in a much less steep arc than it did on your pitch shots, either landing in front of the green and bouncing on or landing on it and rolling well past the hole.

What you want to try to do now is to stop the ball hole-high and as close to the cup as you can. This is basically a "feel" shot, and the way to achieve your goal is to get the right feel for the swing arc and force you need from the distance you are chipping from. Remember, no divots.

So, go through your next 19 balls with the idea of finding the right combination of factors that add up to the right feel for the particular distance you have chosen. Also take into account, if you

Figure 42

are hitting to a level green, that a green that slants toward or away from you will have a different effect on the shot, as will a green that slants in a sidehill fashion.

Once you are able to hit this shot within one-putt range on at least half your 20 balls, move 5 yards closer and run through the drill again, then 5 yards closer than that, and so on, until you are hitting short, straight chips from about 10 yards off the green. By this time you should be able to put each ball within easy one-putt range of the cup, and you might even tick the flagstick with several shots, if not sink one or two.

SEVENTH DRILL

Now for the "cut shot" with the 15 wood. Here you are going to start close to the green and work your way out to greater distances. Drop your first 20 balls on the fairway 10 yards before the open front of the green. This time take the same narrow-footed stance and half-choke grip as before, *but open your address considerably* and *also the face of the club.* (See Fig. 43.)

The idea with this shot, as it is with an iron cut shot, is to swing slightly across the ball in the direction your body is turned, which is well to the left of your target. With the club face in a normal position, such a swing would propel the ball to the left, way off course. But with the club face opened and pointing to the right at address, when it meets the ball it will point straight at the target. (See Fig. 44.) Its opened position provides a considerably higher loft angle at the moment of impact, though less club-head mass. The result: the ball will pop abruptly upward and to the right, toward the target, at the moment of impact, while on your full follow-through the club head will point to the left.

Try the shot. Probably you will not get it right the first few times, but you'll get the idea. Before you can produce a good example of the shot from 10 yards off the green, you will have to adjust your stance and degree of club-face openness several times and also the length of your swing arc and the force you put into the swing. Generally, your swing force should be that of a full 15-wood shot. Start with half swing to see how you do. Once you start hitting good cut shots, you will most likely find it necessary to

Figure 43

Figure 44

further modulate your swing arc to gain consistent distance to the pin, using full force.

Say you are 10 yards from the green and it is another 20 yards to the pin. To get close to the pin with this high but quick-to-stop shot, you will need to hit it 25 yards in the air. Keep practicing through 20, 40, even 60 balls until you can achieve a high cut-shot chip of 25 yards that consistently lands where you want it to.

Note: The downfall of any cut shot, short or long, occurs when the golfer "gives up" on the shot, softening his swing out of uncertainty over his left-of-the-target body alignment. Psychologically, the golfer feels uncomfortable and is afraid of pulling the ball away from the target.

To get the most out of this shot once you've learned the basic principle, you *have to trust it.* Carry through your swing fully, firmly, and intently—perhaps apply even more force than usual at the beginning to ensure the bold force of the swing. Only a forceful, good-tempo swing will make the shot work. Hesitate, or be less than bold with your swing, and the shot will fail. Either it will pop up ineffectually to the right, or it will indeed pull to the left and end up much farther away than you wanted it to go.

You can never practice this shot enough, so run through 40 or 50 additional balls from 10 yards off the green. By the time you're finished you'll have it well in hand. Once you do, retreat 10 yards and run through another 40 balls from this new distance, constantly adjusting your swing arc and force until you are consistently able to put the ball within easy range of the cup.

Then retreat to 30 yards and repeat the routine. Here you are back in the long-chip range. But understand that you are learning the long-chip 15-wood cut shot for reasons different from the straight long chip. The reasons are to get you over hazards and onto the green on long chipping-distance shots, and to get you onto the green out of rough or sand that adjoins the green.

When you can hit at least half of your high, long-chip cut shots with reasonable accuracy, you will be ready to advance to work on the same shots over actual hazards. Remember, all cut shots, short or long, should be completed with a full follow-through in the leftward direction your body is facing. Of course, if you are a left-hander, the rule is reversed insofar as the direction of your follow-through is concerned.

EIGHTH DRILL

This time find a place close to the green that requires you to shoot over a sand trap to get onto the putting surface and near the stick. (See Fig. 45.) Under real conditions you will probably be in the rough, so for this drill drop your first 20 balls in the shortest rough you can find. Now hit 20 short cut shots, this time over the trap and onto the green.

Do you see what I mean? The principle is no different from that of hitting a wedge or 9 iron, though with an iron the shot is much more delicate and difficult than it is with a 15 wood. (Remember, you are still hitting with a half-choke grip.) If you are a typical golfer who has trouble short-chipping over traps and other trouble with an iron to get on the green, you are going to find the 15-wood cut shot the miracle of the ages. Again, you have to put much less effort and "touch" into it than you do with a conventional iron. The 15 wood's unique club head does most of the work. Once

Figure 45

you've grooved the swing this shot calls for, it will become routinely successful.

Move farther away from the trap in five-yard increments and hit 20 to 40 cut shots over the hazard from each distance. When you reach 30 yards' distance you will be thoroughly comfortable with the technique of the shot from any distance and will also have fine-tuned your swing's arc and force. Remember at all times, though, that you never take a divot from any distance. And that you hit all the shots with the half-choke grip and a full follow-through.

NINTH DRILL

Now find a shallow trap next to the green and prepare to learn to turn the cut shot into an effective sandblast. How do you do this? It's simple. You will do everything as you did before. But now you will introduce an additional element into the swing package: hitting into the sand behind the ball.

The question I have heard most often from woodiron doubters is, How can you hit short sand-trap shots with the 15 wood? The principle is no different from that of an ordinary sand iron: you blast through the sand behind the ball and allow the force of the club digging into the sand, and the sand cushion it creates, to propel the ball out of the trap. (See Fig. 46.)

Admittedly, learning the variables of swing force, impact point, and so on takes just as long with a 15 wood as with a sand iron. But once you learn them, the 15 wood has an uncanny way of being more effective and consistent than an ordinary sand wedge.

As I said, start with a shallow trap. Applying the basic stance and swing techniques of the cut shot, try a few blasts. You'll quickly get the idea, particularly the idea of applying greater force to your downswing and of how far behind the ball to strike the sand. You'll soon find your balls popping nicely and gently onto the green.

Next, find a deeper trap and go through the drill again. You will need to apply more force to get the desired loft, but you'll discover how much more in fairly quick order.

Once you've gotten handy at the medium-deep trap shot, find a really deep bunker, whether at your practice hole or at another

Figure 46   *Figure 47*

green on the course—the kind of bunker so deep, and with such a steep bank, that you can't see the flag, much less the green.

Work at 40 to 60 shots out of this hazard. At the beginning you'll find that your balls will pop short into the bank and probably dribble back down into the sand. Keep working, increasing the force of your swing, closing your club face gradually, straightening out your alignment as you go until you are no longer swinging as in the cut-shot chip. You will soon learn that this deep-bunker shot, to be consistently successful, needs a full-face straight-ahead blast, about 2 inches behind the ball, to achieve the loft necessary to get it over the bank and onto the green.

Don't expect to become an expert at these sand shots during this session. All the drill is designed to do is give you a good feel of what you need to do to execute the shots consistently. Once you start playing golf regularly with your woodirons, you will encounter all sorts of adjacent-to-the-green sand-trap situations. You will have to tailor each shot to the depth of the trap and conditions of the sand—hard, soft, or gravelly, wet or dry. Nevertheless, these sand drills will give you a good start toward mastering almost any kind of sand shot with the 15 wood. If by chance you are already a highly proficient sand player with the sand iron, there is probably no need for you to learn to play the 15 wood out of sand. The likelihood is, though, that you are not very proficient with the sand wedge. If you're not, the 15 wood will become your club of choice. It may, however, take longer to learn to use the 15 wood effectively for the infinite variety of sand shots than other more conventional shots. How quickly you learn will depend on how much practice you are willing to put into it.

TENTH DRILL

This is also a sand-trap exercise, but from traps that are at a remove from the green. Almost every golf course has such traps— usually shallow ones. They are anywhere from 25 to 75 yards in front of or off to the sides of the green and are designed to penalize short and/or slightly offline approach shots.

Find such a trap on your course and drop 20 balls onto the sand. The trick here is to hit the ball directly and take a sand divot ahead of the ball, not to hit the sand first. The shot is executed much like a short-to-medium high-flying pitch from grass in which you take a normal 15-wood divot—except that the divot is carved out of sand instead of turf. (See Fig. 47.)

Here you will adjust your grip length, swing arc, and swing force to suit the distance between your lie in the trap and your target on the green. From 25 yards-and-in you will probably want to use a half-choke grip and modulate your swing until you achieve the right distance with each shot. From a trap beyond 25 yards, use a full grip and continue to modulate your swing arc and force until you get a good feel for what you need to put into the shot for any distance under 75 yards. For a shot of more than 75 yards, you will want to go to a lower woodiron. By the time you become thoroughly familiar with all the woodirons, you will be able to hit greens regularly from traps well away, with, say, a 7 wood or 8 wood. Remember that such approaches from distant traps subtract 30 to 40 yards from your normal distance factor for each woodiron.

This is because the sand divot you make after you strike the ball will slow down your follow-through.

In this drill, hit 40 balls from a trap 25 yards away from the green. Then hit another 40 from a trap (if you can find one) about 50 yards away—and, if you can find one, from about 75 yards away. If you find the 75-yard distance too much for your 15 wood, save it until you get to the lower-numbered woodirons.

When you're finished, you will have a thorough grounding in these shots and will be well prepared for any sand hazard you might find during a normal round of golf. Now it's time to go to the next-to-last drill of this afternoon's session.

ELEVENTH DRILL

Here you are going to accustom yourself to hitting cut-shot chips and straight pitches out of the rough to the green from different distances with the 15 wood. Basically, the various shots are the same as those you've already practiced. The only difference will be in your lies.

Start from 10 yards off the green in shallow rough. To execute this shot properly you need to carry out the short cut-shot chip you worked on during the seventh drill: open stance, half grip, open club face, and a swing across the ball with full follow-through. Because of the rough, you will have to apply a bit more arc and force to your swing. Stroke 20 balls or more, until the results indicate that you can put the ball close to the pin on more than half your shots.

Now move 10 yards farther away from the green and hit another 20 to 40 cut shots. Then another 10 yards, and another, until you are used to hitting half-grip, full-swing cut shots from the rough 50 yards away.

Follow this by coming back toward the green with the same series of shots from deeper rough, if you can find it. Deeper rough will slow down your follow-through a bit, so you will probably have to take a bigger swing and apply more force from each distance than you did with cut shots from the shallower rough and fairway. Keep adjusting with each series of shots until you find the right swing, force, and tempo for each distance.

TWELFTH DRILL

Today's final drill is designed to complete your knowledge of the 15 wood's infinite variety. Drop 20 balls at the edge of the green, a foot or two away from the fringe. What you should do here is hit short straight running chips to the flagstick, which may be 20 to 50 feet away. The basic grip and stroke is the one you learned at the start of the morning session, in which you grip the club in a full choke position, extend your forefinger down the outside of the shaft, and use what amounts to a wristy putting stroke. The only rule to remember is that the shorter the chip, the lower down on the handle you should grip the club; and the longer the chip, the higher up you should grip. This will enable you to control your distance on any given just-off-the-green straight-ahead running chip shot, whether out of rough or fringe grass.

The stroke is like a putt's, but not the swing. In other words, do not try to make the shot with a flat, all-arms putting swing. Instead, make it a fully arced swing, crisply and wristily scooping through the ball without taking a divot, while at the same time modulating the length of the arc and force of the stroke to the distance desired. (See Fig. 48.)

The object of the drill is to learn to adjust your stroke to the distance of the chip, all the while maintaining the basic mechanics of the stroke. It is not a cut-shot chip but a straightaway stroke. The longer you have to travel, the higher on the shaft your grip and the longer your stroke should be . (See Fig. 49.) Even with a full grip, though, you should keep your lower forefinger extended down the shaft. This provides marvelous leverage, feel for the shot, and directional stability.

Practice 20 chips each from distances of between 10 feet (extreme choke grip) and 60 feet (full grip). By the time you're finished, you will find that the 15 wood is the most effective chipping tool you have ever had in your hands.

All in all, you have had a full and satisfying day of work with the 15 wood. You have learned at first hand about most of its possibilities and virtues as compared to conventional short irons. If you have time, it might be worth engaging in one final brief drill to drive the point home.

Figure 48   *Figure 49*

Take a conventional pitching wedge and hit 10 balls toward the green with it from your maximum distance for the 15 wood. Then hit 10 balls from the same distance with the 15 wood. If you don't find that your 15-wood shots are much more accurate and consistent than your wedge shots, then you are a pretty good wedge player and should plan to keep that club in your bag.

But if you are like almost everyone I know who has gone from conventional irons to woodirons, your beginning 15-wood shots will be shots that are markedly better and more consistent than any you are able to execute with your pitching or sand wedge. If that's the case, put your wedges away for a while, or at least until you are confronted by a lie (such as being buried in sand) that you simply cannot execute with a 15 wood.

Of course, once you become proficient with all the woodirons, you will rarely find yourself in a situation you can't get out of effectively with your 15 wood.

The second day:
morning session

This morning you are going to play a round of golf. Not a round of golf as you're used to playing it, but a practice round over your own course in which you will carry only your 15 wood and hit every stroke with it, starting from the first tee.

The point is to help you further to groove your basic 15-wood swing and to show you how the club can be used profitably under all sorts of conditions in an actual game of golf. The round will be an extension of what you practiced yesterday afternoon, except that you will be hitting only one ball for each shot, instead of dozens. You will not be putting. Your object will be to get from tee to green on each hole in as few shots as possible, employing only your 15 wood. After you reach each green, you will pick up and proceed to the next tee.

I am not familiar with your golf course and I will not be with you, so of course I cannot instruct you in specific terms on how to play this 15-wood-only practice round. However, I can give you a general idea by showing you how I would guide you if you were playing the round over the course at which I regularly play.

Fig. 50 is a map of my course. I suggest that you mark the map's page because you will be consulting it frequently in the pages

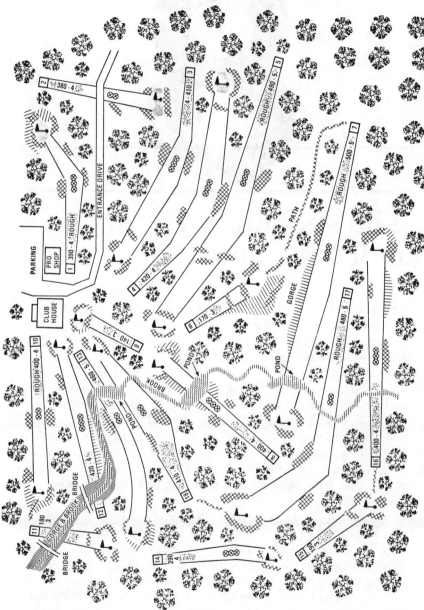

Figure 50

ahead. Let's call the course I have mapped "the Links." Before you go out to play this morning's 15-wood practice round on your own course, I want you to study the map of the Links and then follow me on paper as I play a similar practice round over the first 6 holes of the course, using only a 15 wood. By doing this, you will be able to play your own actual practice round to much greater effect.

Here are the vital statistics for the Links from both the men's and women's tees:

Hole	Yards (Men/Women)	Par	Hole	Yards (Men/Women)	Par
1	390/340	4	10	400/340	4
2	380/320	4	11	180/160	3
3	410/350	4	12	420/330	4
4	420/360	4	13	460/400	5
5	490/420	5	14	290/240	4
6	170/130	3	15	190/160	3
7	500/430	5	16	400/350	4
8	400/340	4	17	480/420	5
9	140/120	3	18	400/370	4

Total Yardage: 6520/5580 **Par:** 72

Now a golf course is much more than the sum of its yardage and par statistics, and you can discern from examining the map that the Links is a fairly difficult course. It is thickly forested between most of its fairways so that the wild hitter is constantly in trouble. Almost every fairway and green is liberally trapped to penalize less than proficient drives, fairway shots, and approaches. There are three ponds strategically placed to do likewise. A deep gorge, a winding brook, and steep drop-offs alongside fairways and greens threaten the golfer on a number of holes. The course's only redeeming factor is that, except for a few holes, it is generally flat, which usually makes for good lies for the straight-hitting golfer.

The first time I played the Links while using only a 15 wood, I kept a detailed scorecard of my progress from tee to green on each hole, as I want you to do when you play your own 15-wood practice round. Of course, like you, I was new to the 15 wood at the time and made plenty of mistakes. Recently I played it again with just a 15 wood for comparison purposes, and this is the way my round went. Follow me as I take you through it, for it will give you a much clearer notion of how to play *your* first practice round.

As a further preface, I should tell you that I am six feet three inches tall, weigh 190 pounds, and can drive a golf ball, using a controlled swing, for an average of 240 yards. Thus I am perhaps a little above average in natural power and length. When I started with woodirons, my maximum distance factor with the 15 wood was 110 yards. Today, as a result of years of use, I have naturally, without forcing my shots, stretched that factor to 130 yards.

HOLE 1: 390 yards: Par 4. As you look at the map, you'll see that the Links' relatively short Par 4 first hole is a dogleg to the left. The fairway is level out to the two driving traps, then proceeds moderately downhill to the green as it angles left. The medium-sized green is open-fronted but well trapped. The ground falls off sharply beyond and between the traps.

I started the round by hitting my 15 wood full and clean off the driving tee for a distance of 130 yards. The straight shot landed me just beyond the point where the rough ends and the actual fairway begins. (*Note:* When using the 15 wood off the tees during your practice round, do not tee the ball up; simply hit "clean" shots off the grass; we will get into hitting teed-up balls with woodirons later.) Hitting my second shot full and clean from the center of the fairway, I carried across the edge of the left-hand driving trap and landed in the left center of the fairway. Because the fairway is downhill here, I got an extra 10 yards for a total yardage of 140, leaving me 120 yards from the center of the green. My third shot was therefore a long pitch-approach to the open-fronted green. I hit a full-swing divot shot. The ball soared straight and true, but I had miscalculated: because of the downhill factor, I got more yardage than I needed. The ball landed toward the back of the green. Thankfully it had plenty of backspin and stopped just before the rear fringe. I was within reasonable two-putt range. *Score: On in 3 strokes.*

HOLE 2: 380 yards: Par 4. Here we have another relatively short par 4, straight but uphill over the entrance drive, beyond which the fairway levels out. Again, a well-trapped medium-sized green, a trap along the right side of the fairway to catch sliced drives, and thick woods on the left to devour hooked or pulled tee shots.

My full, clean 15 wood from the tee would not carry the entrance drive; it landed, 120 yards out on the fairway, about 60 yards short of the drive. My second shot carried 130 yards over the drive to the level fairway, leaving me 130 yards away from the center of the open-fronted green. I hit my approach shot clean; it bounced about 8 yards in front of the putting surface, a little too close for comfort to the right-hand trap, and rolled to a stop in the right-center portion of the green. Again, not one of my better 15-wood shots, but still within two-putt distance. *Score: On in 3.*

HOLE 3: 410 yards: Par 4. A level hole with a slight, gradual bend to the right. Driving traps at 200 yards to swallow errant tee shots, a trap 20 yards in front of the large green to keep approach shots honest, and three traps ringing the green.

My 15-wood shot from the tee ate up 130 yards and landed in the fairway beyond the rough line. I hit my second shot clean and full, spanned another 130 yards, and landed well ahead of the driving traps on the right side of the fairway. But now I faced a problem. If I hit my third 15 wood full and straight, I would probably land in the trap in front of the green, since the distance was about 130 yards. I could have aimed for the left of the trap in the hope of squeezing into the small slice of fairway adjoining it, but I decided it was too risky. So I chose to lay up in front of the sand. I hit a full divot shot straight at the trap, and the ball, getting 110 yards, stopped 15 yards in front. Now I had a 40-yard pitch-approach shot over the trap to the green. I had a choice between hitting a full cut-shot chip or a short, straight, half-swing pitch. I decided on the latter because I had plenty of fairway and green to work with once I lofted the ball over the trap (see map). My shot carried nicely over the trap, hit about 5 yards in front of the green, and rolled to a stop 4 feet from the pin. *Score: On in 4.*

HOLE 4: 420 yards: Par 4. A look at the Links map will show you that this hole is pretty much a repeat of hole 3, except that it bends slightly to the left. I played it much the same as I did the previous hole. *Score: On in 4.*

HOLE 5: 490 yards: Par 5. Except for the fact that this level hole is a par 5 at 490 yards, it is not unlike hole 3. The main difference is the three fairway traps between 380 and 410 yards from the tee, designed to punish less-than-excellent fairway-wood second shots after long drives. A top-notch golfer should carry these traps easily with his second shot, setting himself up for a simple pitch approach to the large, trap-encircled green.

I played two full 15 woods for my first two shots, getting a total distance down the fairway of 260 yards. I could not carry the fairway traps with my third shot, so I laid up with a full divot shot that left me 10 yards in front of the closest trap. Now I was faced with a shot to the center of the green, over the trap guarding its front edge (see map) of 120 yards. This was risky, since my maximum distance factor with the 15 wood is only 130 yards. If I hit a full divot shot I would probably end up in the front trap. I would need a perfectly struck, full, clean 15-wood pitch shot to put me on the green. I decided to go for it, sternly reminding myself not to overswing or otherwise try to force the shot. Alas, I didn't force it; instead, I was overcome by doubt as I came into my downswing. As a result, I let up. Although I hit the ball well and straight, it only traveled 90 yards. Nevertheless it stopped before it could roll into the front green trap. For my fifth shot I hit a choke-grip cut chip over the trap and onto the green, 3 feet from the pin. *Score: On in 5.*

HOLE 6: 170 yards. Par 3. A straight hole but very difficult for anyone who cannot hit and hold the green on the tee shot. The ground along the right of the short fairway, and immediately adjacent to the right of the green, falls off sharply in a steep bank of thick rough. The traps in front and to the left of the green are deep, and a too-powerful recovery shot out of them will run the ball over the green and down the bank. Also there's an intermediate trap exactly 130 yards from the tee to catch topped or popped-up tee shots.

A full, clean 15-wood shot from the tee would have put my

ball squarely in this trap. So I hit a high full divot shot to stop 10 yards in front. My second shot, therefore, was a 50 yarder that I had to loft over the trap in front of the green without running the ball over the far bank. I stroked a half-choke, three quarter-swing divot pitch that just carried the trap, bouncing on the green's front fringe and rolling to a stop 7 feet beyond the pin. I was safe. *Score: On in 2.*

Having followed me over the first six holes of the Links as I played them with a 15 wood alone, you can perceive the value of such an unorthodox practice round. The basic idea is to concentrate on the various strokes you have learned with the 15 wood, execute them as best you can in the face of changing course conditions and psychological pressures, and try to maintain a reasonable tee-to-green score.

I think you'll be amazed by how well you score using only your 15 wood. When I finished my round, this was my tee-to-green tally:

Hole	Yards	Par	My Score (tee-to-green no putts)	Hole	Yards	Par	My Score (tee-to-green no putts)
1	390	4	3	10	400	4	4
2	380	4	3	11	180	3	2
3	410	4	4	12	420	4	4
4	420	4	4	13	460	5	4
5	490	5	5	14	290	4	3
6	170	3	2	15	190	3	2
7	500	5	4	16	400	4	3
8	400	4	3	17	480	5	4
9	140	3	2	18	400	4	4
				Total:		72	60

Par for the Links is 72. I had a tee-to-green score of 60. Add to that an average of two putts per green, or 36 additional strokes. Had I been putting and been able to get the ball down in an average of two putts per hole, my total score, using only a 15 wood and putter, would have been 96, or 24 over par. You and I know many golfers who can't shoot 96 with a full bag of clubs, no less a single club. Perhaps even you are such a golfer.

To be sure, I don't expect you to go out on your first 15-wood practice round and make a tee-to-green score of 60. In the first place, you are still too new to the 15 wood and are a few days away from feeling totally confident in all its capabilities. Second, your course may be more difficult than the Links. If it's easier, naturally you have a good chance of coming in closer to a 60 from tee to green.

But your score is not the central concern of your first practice round; it is only an incentive, something to make the round more interesting. The basic object is to put you on a golf course with only a 15 wood and see what happens. Without putting, you should be able to play the round in about two and a half hours if you are walking, less if you use a cart. If you are particularly adventurous, you might follow it up with an identical round using only a conventional wedge. I'm certain you'll find that you score even higher, tee to green, with your familiar wedge iron than with the not-yet-familiar 15 wood (or, as some of its proponents call it, the "wedgewood").

In order to benefit most fully from the practice round you are about to play, keep the following points firmly in mind:

1. All tee shots from the grass. Clean, full swing strokes based on what you learned yesterday on the practice range—grip, stance, address, a good-tempo swing in order to achieve your natural distance with the club, full follow-through.

2. Same with all fairway and rough shots that are farther away from the green than your maximum distance factor with the 15 wood.

3. When you look out from tee or fairway to distant greens you'll be surveying considerable distances, which might give you the urge to powder the ball as far as you can. Resist the urge! The 15 wood is not a distance club, and all you'll do is mis-hit it. Instead, concentrate on grooving your swing for your natural maximum distance factor. You will have the opportunity to get more distance later with other clubs.

4. When you get within one-shot distances of the greens, start planning your shots based on distance, hazards, winds (if any), lie, uphill or downhill, and so on. Consider different possible shots (full divot shots, half-choke clean shots, half-swing full-grip shots, cut shots, running chips). Then choose the shot you think is best and stick with it.

5. If shooting out of sand or rough, adjust your shot as required by the conditions and in accordance with what you learned during yesterday's practice.

6. Finally, at all times take this practice round seriously. Concentrate fully on each shot. Vow to stay down on each shot, trying not to overswing or force it.

If you can carry out all these precepts, I guarantee that as you go along you will find yourself hitting more and more pretty shots—long approaches, short pitches, straight and cut-chip shots, even sand recoveries.

The second day: afternoon session

Now it's back to the practice range. Why? Because you have played your first practice round with the 15 wood and things did not go as well as they might have. You flubbed a tee shot here, a fairway shot there; you hit a pitch shot too weakly here, a chip too strongly there; you blew a cut shot here, a sandblast there. You need more work, more fine tuning, with the 15 wood before you progress to the lower-numbered woodirons.

FIRST DRILL

So, back to the practice range for an hour with 100 or more balls. You are going to play the round you played this morning—but this time in your head, so to speak. Warm up with 10 full-swing shots, half clean and half divot. Now you are ready to go to work.

Put a ball down on the tee and imagine it's your first shot of your morning round, off your course's first tee. Think about it for a moment. Think about what you did wrong during the morning to make the first shot of your practice round a less than ideal full 15-wood shot. Maybe you pulled or pushed it off the fairway. Maybe you yanked yourself up and topped it. Maybe you hit it fat and short.

Whatever you did wrong, it was undoubtedly due to tension—over your unfamiliarity with the 15 wood, over the distance to the green that confronted you, perhaps even over the fact that people were watching you.

But now you are back in the relaxed atmosphere of the practice tee. There is no green 300 or 400 yards distant to spook you. There are no people gazing at you curiously; everyone else is busy with his or her own practice shots. So relax, think calmly about what went wrong, and then stroke a full-swing clean 15-wood shot toward a target you have set out at your maximum distance.

There—wasn't that better? Now, pick out the spot where your ball came to rest and equate it visually in your mind with a spot on the first fairway of your course. Put down another ball and imagine you are hitting your second shot from that visualized spot. Think about what the actual shot demands—clean or divot, full swing or half swing or other, and so on. And think about and visualize what you would be shooting at and trying to avoid if you were playing an actual second shot from the spot you've visualized on your first fairway.

Now, with the image firmly in place, set yourself up to the ball and calmly execute the shot.

There again—wasn't that better than this morning?

If the first hole you played this morning was, say, a long par 4, your two opening shots here have left you with a long approach to the green for your third shot. Again, visualize the shot you need to make. Then drop another ball on the practice tee and, gauging the required distance, direction, and loft in your head, execute the desired shot.

As you've played the hole in your imagination, you have probably gotten on the green in 3. See how easy it is? Then why didn't you do it this morning? The answer is that you hadn't yet learned to trust your 15 wood implicitly.

Now, go over this morning's second hole again in your head, replaying each shot from the practice tee as you do. See? The 15 wood is much more faithful and obedient when you are relaxed and trusting than it is when you allow the golf course to boss it, and you, around.

Continue to replay the rest of the morning's round from the

practice tee, using the remainder of your balls to execute each shot. By the time you've gone through the 18 imaginary holes, your 15 wood will be behaving well and consistently. And your confidence in it will begin, finally, to mature. Yes, you'll still hit an occasional flubbed practice tee shot, but it will be nothing like this morning. You will have learned the lesson that I have already preached several times in the preceding pages, but that only a session on the golf course itself with the 15 wood (or any other club, for that matter) can drive home with lasting personal effect. The lesson is: the club will do the work it is designed to do if only you will let it.

SECOND DRILL

After you've finished with the stationary replay of your morning's practice round, work through an additional 50 balls—alternating full-swing clean shots with full-swing divot shots, and hitting at targets you've set up out on the range to correspond with your maximum distance factor for each of the two types of shots.

If your mean distance factor is 100 yards on clean shots, it should be 10 to 20 yards less on divot shots. Increase the figures proportionately if you are a stronger hitter, decrease them if a weaker hitter.

But now, in this drill really try to zero in on your two targets with each alternating shot. At first you'll be well off the mark— short, long, wide. But as you groove yourself into the drill, you'll find that more and more balls drop close to each target. Continue through another 50 balls, or until you are satisfied that you're able to come close on almost every shot—say, 15 yards. Now you are learning to use your 15 wood with long-distance precision, and it should give you a huge boost in morale. Could you possibly execute such shots so frequently with a conventional wedge? I doubt it.

Don't hit so many balls that you tire yourself out, though, and start getting sloppy. You still have a few drills left before you finish the session.

THIRD DRILL

Leave the practice tee and go to the practice green with 40 balls. Drop the balls about 5 yards off the green and start hitting straight, half-in-the-air, half-roll chips to the stick. Stay at the drill until you can put at least half your shots within 3 feet of the cup.

FOURTH DRILL

Establish yourself in low rough about 10 yards from a good-sized sand trap separating you from the green. From here, practice a few dozen high cut-shot chips over the trap and onto the green. You probably blew a few of these during the morning round.

After you've completed this drill, go out on your course and find an elevated green that has a trap at its foot, so that you have to cut-chip not only over the trap but the high bank fronting the green. Again, work on several dozen such shots from this depressed position. (See Fig. 51.)

Then find a spot where the opposite factors come into play—where you're hitting over a trap from a level well above the green.

Figure 51   *Figure 52*

Practice a generous number of cut chips from this position. (See Fig. 52.)

The idea with all these difficult and diverse shots is, as with a conventional wedge, to get the ball high into the air immediately, with the proper distance, direction, and backspin. To make these shots consistently with a 15 wood is no less difficult than with a conventional wedge, at least at the beginning. But as I have said earlier, once you become proficient at them, you will find them easier and consistently far more rewarding with your 15 wood than with your wedge. As every golfer knows, they are the game's most common trouble shots, and the ordinary player who can master them will often save 4, 5 or more strokes a round.

FIFTH DRILL

For the final drill of the afternoon, go to the shallowest trap you can find adjoining a green—one with only a minimal lip between you

Figure 53

and the pin. (See Fig. 53.) Hit 10 straight chips from the trap, barely brushing the sand and letting the club face scoop the ball into the air—just as you would with a short running chip from grass. Then hit 10 blast cut shots, modulating the force of your swing to accommodate the distance between you and the pin. (Remember to strike the sand well behind the ball, as you would with a sand iron.)

When you're finished, survey the results. Which was the consistently more effective shot, the delicate chip or the forceful blast? This exercise will tell you how you can best use your 15 wood in such shallow-trap situations. If you find the chip more comfortable and effective, plan on perfecting that as your shot of choice for such situations. If on the other hand you find the blast technique better suited to you, then plan to work on this as your standard shot.

Finish the drill by hitting a few dozen more balls from the trap, using the shot you have settled on.

You have by now learned and practiced a wide variety of golf shots the 15 wood—the key club of the Woodiron Method—is capable of. Although perhaps initially discouraged, particularly by your practice round of this morning, you can not help but be impressed by the club's ease, function, and potential.

Sufficiently impressed to want to continue to learn the Woodiron Method? If you are an average golfer to whom conventional irons remain the biggest source of complaint, I think so.

But this is the time to make up your mind. For if you intend to continue, you must now acquire your second woodiron—the 10 wood. This is what you'll be working with in tomorrow's sessions.

10

The third day: morning session: the 10 wood

Now that you possess a 10 wood, compare it to your conventional 6 iron, of which it is the equivalent. (See Fig. 54.) The first thing you'll notice, aside from the obvious club-head difference, is that the 10 wood has a shaft that is 2 to 3 inches longer than the 6 iron's. The difference is one that runs through the entire series of woodirons as compared to their iron equivalents. It is one of the two key factors that make the woodirons easier and more effective clubs to play with.

With the longer shaft, you are able to set yourself up to the ball in a more natural fashion and achieve a more generous swing arc without losing any precision. The longer shafts, in fact, nicely counterbalance the heavier, bulkier club heads of the woodirons. Because of this, at the moment of impact you get the effect of a perfectly struck iron without having to make the swing adjustments needed to strike an iron perfectly. This is the engineering secret of the woodirons.

On those few occasions when you hit an ideal 6-iron shot, how far does it go—100 yards, 120 yards, 140 yards, 160 yards? Whatever your potential maximum distance with a 6 iron is, that's the distance you can expect to achieve regularly with your 10 wood—

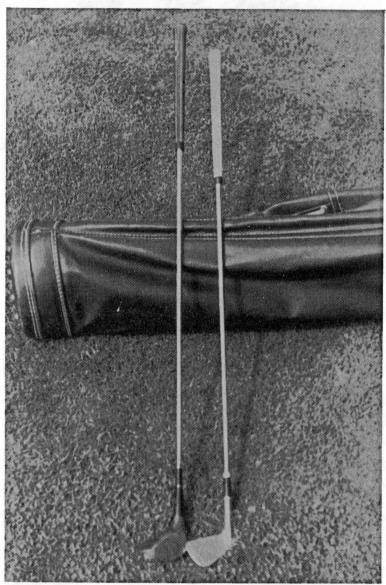

Figure 54

high, straight shots that carry a good piece of ground and look as if they've come right off the pro tour.

Another way to gauge your probable beginning distance factor with the 10 wood is to measure it against the maximum distance factor you have established for your 15 wood during the past two days. Simply add 40 yards to your 15-wood distance factor and you'll arrive at a rough approximation of the distance you should be able to achieve with the 10 wood to start. Of course, if your 15-wood distance factor gradually lengthens as you further use the woodirons, so too should your 10-wood distance.

Thus, if your present 15-wood distance factor is 100 yards, you can expect to start hitting shots of 140 yards with your 10 wood right off. If your 15-wood factor is 120 yards, you can look for 10-wood shots of 160 yards—the moderately powerful golfer's average distance with his 6 iron.

This morning's session sends you back to the practice tee. But before you go, take the 10 wood in your hands and wiggle it around to get a feel of its heft and balance. Now take a few relaxed three-quarter practice swings on the grass, letting the bottom of the club head just brush the ground. See how good and natural it feels?

Now swing a few times with your 6 iron. Then switch back to the 10 wood and swing it a few more times. Finally, compare the feel of the two clubs. I think you'll agree that the sensation of the 6 iron can't hold a candle to that of the 10 wood.

Time to go to the practice tee, then. Take your 15 wood, 10 wood and plenty of balls.

FIRST DRILL

Don't touch the 10 wood yet. This is warm-up time, and I want you to warm up with about 25 shots using the 15 wood. Start with a few short full-choke chips to get the feel of the club again, then gradually work up to full-grip, full-swing clean and divot shots. Concentrate on stance, address, swing-tempo, and force. Don't stop the warm-up drill until you're hitting most of your long 15-wood shots close to where you want them to land.

SECOND DRILL

Now switch to your 10 wood. But before you start, listen to a few more words about the club.

The 10 wood, like the 6 iron, is a club designed for a number of uses. It is designed for straight approach shots of certain yardages onto the green, and for tee shots to the green on par-3 holes of certain yardages. It is designed for long shots out of rough toward or onto the green. It is designed for long shots toward or onto the green from fairway traps. It is designed for long shots that have to carry over hazards to get you close to, or onto, the green. And it is designed to provide long lay-up shots when needed.

Of course, all the other woodirons are designed to do the same things—specific distance being the differentiating factor between one and the next. The same is true for the conventional irons, naturally. Again, the principal difference between the irons and the woodirons is that with the latter, almost all of the above potentials are easier to achieve consistently for the average golfer— you, me—than they are with the former.

The 10 wood should be approached no differently, basically, than the 15 wood. Your swing with the 10 wood will always be a full swing with a full grip—such as your swing when hitting long, clean 15-wood shots. The only thing you'll do differently is the manner in which you take your stance. Because the 10 wood's shaft is considerably longer than the 15 wood's, you will naturally take your stance a little farther away from the ball. Otherwise, everything is the same. Address the ball so that it is forward of the center line of your body, as with the 15 wood. And when you swing, follow the mechanics of your basic 15-wood swing, which by now should be well etched in your muscle memory.

There are two slightly different shots you will hit with the 10 wood, and they are comparable to the two basic long-distance 15-wood shots you have learned. The first is the full-swing clean shot in which you strike the ball off the turf without taking a divot. The other is the full-swing divot shot.

The reason for the two different shot techniques should be clear from examining your 10 wood's club face and metal soleplate. Like the 15 wood, the soleplate angles upward a fraction into the surface of the club face, leaving a sharp cutting edge at the angle. Whenever a ball lies hugging the surface of the turf—on a tightly manicured fairway, for instance—you will want to take a slight divot to ensure that the soleplate is under the ball at the moment of impact. When a ball lies on coarser fairway grass, or in rough itself, you can skip the divot because there is enough of a cushion between the ball and ground to enable the soleplate to get under the ball.

Now to the second drill. Start by putting a few balls down and addressing each. Then take a series of lazy half swings, letting the club head strike each ball—almost as if you were chipping. This will give you your first feel of the 10-wood contact and enable you to adjust your stance and address until you find the most comfortable alignment.

After a few of these casual hits, start gradually to firm up your swing and lengthen it, concentrating on tempo, increasing force, staying down on the ball and follow-through. Hit about 20 balls, not worrying about where they go, until you begin to feel a swing groove develop. Remember, your object here is to strike the ball at the bottom of your arc and let the force and timing of your swing, plus the angle of the club face, propel the ball up and away.

Once you begin to feel the groove settle in, start following the flight of each shot. If they are flying generally straight and at least as far as your 15-wood shots, you are in good shape. If not, continue to make adjustments in stance, grip, and swing mechanics until they do.

THIRD DRILL

Once you're able to propel the ball reasonably straight, high, and far, you are ready to refine and firm up the force of your full swing for maximum distance and optimum loft and direction. (The desired 10-wood shot, like that of the 6 iron, is high; because of the diminished loft angle, it is not as high as the 15 wood, though.)

To do this, put down 20 balls in a row, as in earlier drills. Approach each ball as though it were a vital shot during a real round of golf. Proceed to hit through the 20 balls, taking your time before each shot to make sure that everything about your setup is correct. As you swing and strike at each ball, put as much force as you can into the stroke *without exceeding your best tempo*; in other words, try to hit the ball as hard as you can without overswinging or forcing the shot.

The key to this drill is club-head speed. What you are trying to do now is to combine the mechanics of your swing, including the action of your legs and torso as they move through the ball, to produce maximum controlled club-head speed at the impact moment. You achieve this not by overswinging, not through exaggerated hip thrust, not by consciously "racing" the club head through the ball, but by the smoothness, rhythm, and balance of your swing—the factors that add up to good tempo and timing. So—concentrate in this drill on hitting your 10 wood with force but with reasonable swing tempo. Always keep your swing "within yourself"; if you go too fast you will break up your tempo and balance and, more often than not, botch the shot.

Find the right tempo with the first 20 balls, then drop another 20. Run deliberately but aggressively through them, this time grooving the tempo you have found best suited to you. Once you are able to lock the correct tempo into your body's muscle memory, you will have found the swing you will use with all the woodirons. It will be the swing you will apply as well to your regular woods, including your driver.

At the end of this drill, you will have seen once again how effectively woodirons do the work when you swing correctly. You are now ready to begin reaching for your maximum distance factor with the 10 wood.

FOURTH DRILL

Walk out on the range and set up a target in the general area of where the majority of your shots of the last drill landed. Then pace off the distance back to where you've been hitting from the practice tee. This is your beginning maximum distance factor. It may be only 20 or 30 yards longer than your 15-wood distance factor. Or 40 or 50 yards. If it's less than 40, don't worry; you will begin to get more length as you become more accustomed to the club.

In this drill, hit 40 balls with the 10 wood, maintaining your swing groove and aiming for your target. Most of your shots, if hit cleanly, will end up in an area 10 to 20 yards beyond a line drawn laterally through your target. You are now settling in on your final maximum distance factor with the 10 wood.

Move your target to the new distance line. Pace off the distance back to the tee. Now, hit 20 more balls aimed at the new target distance, further refining the groove and tempo of your swing as you come closer and closer with each shot.

FIFTH DRILL

Now to the 10-wood divot shot, which you'll want to use on tightly manicured fairways and in other lies in which the ball sits snug to the ground.

The trick on this shot is the same as it is with the 15 wood—to get the bottom leading edge of the club face sufficiently under the ball at impact so that the ball is struck on the club face just above the metal soleplate. The principle of the shot is no different from that of a clean shot off a slight cushion of grass. With the latter, the soleplate at the bottom of the club face naturally gets under the ball, cutting through the grass beneath it. When you are faced with a tight, uncushioned lie, you simply want to force the soleplate under the ball. This means taking a slight divot in the instant after the ball is struck. Not the "blast"-type or massive divot you see many good golfers take with a conventional mid-iron. Simply a shallow concave divot.

The swing for the divot shot is no different from what it is for the clean shot. All you do is go down on the ball a few millimeters more—always making sure that your club head strikes the ball before it makes contact with the ground.

Try a dozen divot shots with the 10 wood. As with the 15 wood, they will probably feel awkward at first and you'll mis-hit a few. Run through another 20 shots or so until you begin to get the idea and your divot shots start to fly straight and high. You will find that such shots travel a shorter distance—10 to 20 yards shorter than the maximum distance factor you established in the last drill for clean shots. That's all right. You will find, once you are playing with all the woodirons, that if you have to make a divot shot to cover your 10 wood's maximum distance, you can simply use a club one or two numbers lower. For instance, depending on your natural hitting power, an 8- or 9-wood divot shot will travel as high and far as a 10-wood clean shot, and will have more backspin in the bargain.

SIXTH DRILL

Set up a second target in the distance area where most of your good divot shots landed, leaving your maximum distance target in place. Then go back to the tee and hit 40 balls, alternating clean shots to the longer target and divot shots to the shorter one.

SEVENTH DRILL

Here you proceed to tee shots with the 10 wood. As I have said, once you are able to hit with this club from anywhere between 130 and 170 yards, you will be able to use it, and its adjoining-numbered woodirons, very effectively for tee shots on most par-3 holes.

I prefer not to use a wooden tee when hitting a woodiron as a tee shot. It gets no more distance than an ordinary clean shot off a cushion of grass, and in fact can reduce yardage by soaring higher, and therefore shorter, than an ordinary grass shot. When I use a woodiron off a par-3 driving tee, I position my ball on a generous cushion of grass and hit it clean from there.

Many converts to woodirons insist on using tees, however, believing that they provide, if nothing else, a psychological edge. You are going to have to make up your own mind about it. But if you choose to employ tees, make sure you tee the ball as low as you can. When you hit a ball with a woodiron off a wooden tee, the bottom of the ball *must still be in solid contact* with the top of the grass. If it is any higher, or if there is air between grass and ball, you are certain to hit the ball much higher and shorter than you want to. (See Fig. 55.)

In this drill, stroke 20 10-wood shots with balls teed up low, as described above. (You will need plenty of wooden tees, since the woodirons' sharp leading edges tend to slice the tops off the deeply

Figure 55

embedded tees.) You will probably find yourself pulling or pushing each ball offline, which provides the second lesson of teed-up woodiron shots. Because of the elevation of the ball, some of you may find it hard to stay down on it; the natural tendency is to pull the club head *up* to meet the ball at the impact moment. This up-pulling motion imparts an excessive leftward (or rightward, if you are left-handed) rotation to your body, flattening out the plane of your swing and follow-through. The result, usually, is pulled shots.

If you find that you have this problem but still want to hit off wooden tees, it is easy to solve. Simply adjust your stance and address slightly forward, so that the ball is an inch or so rearward of where it usually is when you play a normal woodiron shot. This will discourage your tendency to come up on all your teed-up woodiron shots.

Practice more teed-up shots until you find the right address relationship between yourself and the ball. Then begin to aim and measure your shots with respect to your 10 wood's maximum-distance target. Hit another 20 teed-up balls to refine your shots. If you still find them falling 10 to 20 yards short of your maximum distance, you will have a choice: not to tee up your tee shots on par-3 holes, or, later, to use a lower-numbered woodiron. The final decision can wait, however.

EIGHTH DRILL

For this final drill of the morning, you are going to practice par-3 shots with your 10 wood under more realistic conditions than hitting at a practice-range target provides. By now you have a clear idea of your 10 wood's maximum distance factor on both clean turf shots and teed-up shots. Calculate the average between the two. Based on the average yardage you arrive at, go out to your golf course with your 10 wood and 40 balls and find the par-3 hole that is closest in distance to your average yardage. Set yourself up on the tee and start firing carefully thought-out shots at the green, alternating between teed-up shots and clean shots from the turf.

Here you'll begin to get a good picture of the potential of the woodirons for actual par-3 play. Yes, you'll put a few balls into the sand traps ringing the green; yes, you'll even press too much on an occasional shot and pop it up or angle it offline. But I'll bet that at least a third of your balls land and stop on the green.

The quirks and inconsistencies can be worked out over the next few days. What's important is that you will experience a number of beautiful shots, shots that will convince you of the potential of woodirons to set you up for consistent pars and birdies on par-3 holes, rather than the bogeys and double bogeys you are accustomed to getting when you use conventional irons.

Retrieve your balls, go back to the tee, and repeat the drill again. This time really focus in mind and body on putting every shot onto the green. You won't, of course, but your percentage will rise from a third to well over a half. Don't hesitate to let that good feeling wash over you when you see a ball leap off your 10 wood, soar gracefully over a distance of 100 to 160 yards, and settle onto the green within two-putt range of the pin. The more you revel in such shots, the quicker your confidence in the club and your swing will grow. And the more frequently you'll find yourself executing such shots during the next few days, both with the 10 wood and with the other woodirons.

Take one final round of 40 tee shots on the par-3 tee you are working from. By this time you should have settled the question of whether teed-up shots or shots from the turf serve you better. Choose the one you prefer and work through your 40 balls, using only that shot.

The third day: afternoon session

It's back to the golf course this afternoon for another practice round—this time with your 10 wood, 15 wood, *and* putter. On this round you are going to do the following:

1. Hit all shots from tee to green that are at or beyond your 10-wood maximum distance factor with your 10 wood.

2. Hit all shots that are less than your 10-wood distance factor with your 15 wood.

3. Putt out each green and keep a score for the entire round.

The purpose of this round is to further hone your new 10- and 15-wood skills under actual course conditions, and also to keep your concentration focused by giving you a scoring incentive. In other words, you are going to play a serious 18 holes of golf. With the average of 40 or so additional yards per shot provided by the addition of your 10 wood, you will have an opportunity to get onto many greens in one shot less than you did when you played the previous practice round with your 15 wood alone. Thus, if you are able to execute mostly good 10- and 15-wood shots on this round, you should definitely achieve a score that is lower than the scores you are used to shooting, even with a full bag of conventional irons.

Before you start the round, however, take another tour with me around my own golf course, the Links. You'll recall that when I played this course with only a 15 wood, it took me three shots to get onto the green of the 390-yard par-4 first hole. Take a look at how I did when I played it again with the addition of my 10 wood.

I hit my 10 wood off the tee of the first hole without teeing it up, concentrating on a smooth but forceful swing. The shot carried 160 yards to the center of the fairway (see map). My second 10-wood shot rolled to a stop 170 yards farther down the fairway, leaving me with a 15-wood approach to the open-fronted green of only 60 yards, as opposed to the 120-yard shot I was faced with during my previous 15-wood-only round. I used a half-choke pitch-and-run technique for this 60-yarder, landing the ball 10 yards in front of the green and rolling it up to within 4 feet of the pin. I sank the putt for a total score of 4—a par!

I played the second hole, almost identical in yardage, in much the same manner. Because the first half of the hole is uphill, I lost about 15 yards from my 10-wood distance factor on my tee shot, though, and was left with an 80-yard 15-wood approach for my third shot. I got on with a high pitch and two-putted for a total score of 5.

On the 410-yard par-4 third hole, I was on the green in three and one-putted for another par.

On the 420-yard par-4 fourth hole, I made a mistake on my 100-yard 15-wood approach shot, pushing it to the right. Although the ball hit the green, it rolled into the rear of the medium-deep right-hand trap. A 15-wood blast out of the trap and two putts gave me a double-bogey 6.

On the 490-yard par-5 fifth hole, three solid 10-wood shots carried me over the fairway traps and left me 20 yards short of the green's front guard trap. I hit a nicely lofted cut chip over the trap to within 2 feet of the cup. My one-putt gave me a total score of par 5 for the hole.

The 170-yard par-3 sixth hole was too long for my 10 wood, so I played off the tee as I did last time—with my 15-wood—and took a score of 4.

On the 500-yard par-5 seventh hole, my first two 10-wood

shots put me 320 yards out from the tee. But I was still about 140 yards from the 30-yard-wide pond that crosses the fairway (see map). To get over the pond would prove too much for my 10 wood, so I laid up safely with a 15-wood divot shot. From 15 yards in front of the pond, I had a 90-yard pitch to the open-fronted green. I got on easily with my 15 wood, stopping the ball within 8 feet of the pin. It took me two putts to get down, for a one-over-par 6.

On the eighth hole (see map), a straight par-4 of 400 yards with a fairly steep uphill approach to the green from the far edge of the pond, two full 10-wood shots would have put me in the pond. So after my 160-yard 10 wood off the tee, I laid up in front of the pond with a full divot 15-wood second shot of about 110 yards. This left me with a shot of 130 yards across the pond and up the hill to the center of the green. Thus for my third shot I hit a full divot 10 wood, taking into account the fact that the divot, plus the elevation of the green, would reduce my distance factor to about 130 yards. Everything worked as planned, except that I got a few yards less than I'd calculated. My ball bounced 5 yards short of the green and stopped on the front fringe. A 15-wood running chip left me within one-putt distance. I made the putt for a bogey 5.

The ninth hole is a 140-yard par 3 to another elevated green with a deep, yawning bunker in front. The height of the green stretches out the actual tee-shot distance to about 155 yards. I hit a clean 10-wood tee shot that flew straight to the flag and came to a stop about six feet behind the cup. Alas, I left the tricky first putt a few inches short and had to settle for a score of par 3.

Here, then, was my score on the first nine holes, using only a 10 wood, 15 wood, and putter:

Hole	Par	Score	Hole	Par	Score
1	4	4	6	3	4
2	4	5	7	5	6
3	4	4	8	4	5
4	4	6	9	3	3
5	5	5		Par: 36	Total: 42

I managed to play the second nine in one stroke less, thanks to three lucky one-putts, for a score of 41. My total for the round, then, was 83, just 11 over par for the course. And this with just a 10 wood, a 15 wood, and a putter! I had never been able to break 85 before with a full set of conventional clubs. Yet here I was shooting an 83 with just two woodirons and a putter.

At the time I played this round, my handicap on the Links course was 25. Which meant that my average score, playing with conventional irons, was 97. Yet I'd shot an 83, which amounted to a handicap of 11. In one round of golf, using but three clubs, I had cut my handicap by more than half!

A fluke? I was the first to think it was. But then I played several more such rounds. And I repeated my remarkable scoring, more or less. The next time, due to some sloppy putting and two poor 15-wood shots, I came in with an 87. But the round after that I tallied 84. Then 82. Then 85.

Five successive rounds of 83, 87, 84, 82, and 85. Average them out and you get a mean score of 84.5. Which meant for me a new handicap, on the par-72 Links course, of 12.5. Measured against my former handicap of 25, this meant that I had cut my handicap in half—in only a few days.

I won't guarantee that you'll do as well today. I *will* guarantee, though, that if you put your all into your round, you will score considerably lower than you're used to doing with a full bag of conventional clubs. If you are an average-85 golfer, I predict that you'll break 80. If you're an average-95 golfer, you'll come in at about 85, give or take a stroke or two. If you are an average-105 golfer, man or woman, you'll score in the low-to-mid 90s.

If you fail to achieve such a remarkable reduction in your average score, it will only be because you didn't really apply yourself. So, as you set out on this second practice round with your 10 wood, 15 wood, and putter, give it your all in terms of determination and concentration. Remember and apply everything you've learned about the woodirons so far. Think out each shot so that you get the most out of it, while at the same time you stay out of trouble. And use your putter to optimum effect. When I say "give your all," I don't mean, of course, pressing or forcing your shots. Let your two woodirons do the work and trust them to give you the maximum distance and direction you need on any given shot.

12

The fourth day: morning session: the 5 wood

Many of you probably have been using a woodiron for years without realizing it. Although all golf irons were made of wood when the game first started, the 5 wood was the first of the modern woodirons.

Originally the 5 wood was designed as a handy substitute for golfers who found it impossible to play with the 1 and 2 irons. Although classified for many years as a utility wood, its burgeoning popularity has transformed it into a regulation club today. Indeed, 5 woods are included as standard equipment in many matched wood sets sold by golf-club manufacturers.

Very few modern golfers do not carry a 5 wood. Naturally, if you already have a 5 wood, you will not need to purchase one. But if you don't, get one. They are sold separately as well as being included as part of matched sets.

The loft angle of the 5 wood's club face falls roughly between that of the 1 and 2 iron. As with all the woodirons, it has a slightly longer shaft than its iron equivalents. It is, of course, meant to be swung like a wood. When struck properly, it will produce shots of comparatively great distances—anywhere from 150 yards in the hands of a short-hitting golfer to 230 yards in the hands of a powerful pro.

You no doubt already know the distance you are capable of getting with a well-struck 5 wood. But in case you don't, have another look at the woodiron distance chart on page 30. This will give you an idea of what you can expect in terms of distance from your 5 wood. You can also determine it by the maximum distance factor you established yesterday for your 10 wood. If you hit the 10 wood consistently 120 yards, you can expect to get 160 yards from your 5 wood. If your 10-wood distance factor is 140 yards, you should be able to produce shots of 180 yards with your 5 wood. If your 10-wood factor is 160 yards, then figure on 200 yards for your 5 wood. In other words, no matter what your 10-wood factor is, simply add 40 yards to arrive at your probable 5-wood distance factor with a controlled swing.

You may find later that you are capable of hitting the 5 wood 50 or 60 yards farther than the 10 wood. But this is something you really do not want to do, since it will mean that you are putting too much effort into your shots—the kind of effort that causes over-swings and wild shots. You may occasionally get a longer 5 wood, but much more often than not you will end up losing distance.

The 5 wood, like all the other woodirons, will consistently do the work it is designed to do only if you hit the ball with the maximum force you are capable of applying to it *while swinging under control.* To produce that consistency, the first thing you must do is learn to stop thinking of the 5 wood as a fairway club from which you must always try to get the maximum distance possible. You must begin to think of it instead as a woodiron, a club that will give you fairly precise distance and accuracy—at the long end of your personal woodiron distance spectrum—each time you use it. If you can sometimes hit the 5 wood 200 yards, say, with good loft and placement, you should plan on reducing your distance expectations as you begin to make the club an integral part of your woodiron arsenal instead of just another fairway wood. Think now in terms of 180 yards, with even better loft and placement, consistently, rather than 200 yards occasionally.

FIRST DRILL

With all this in mind, you are ready to begin adapting your 5 wood to your overall woodiron game. Go to the practice tee with your 5 wood, 10 wood, and 15 wood. But do not start hitting with the 5 wood yet.

In this initial drill, you should warm up first with your 15 wood, starting with quarter-swing shots and working up to full-swing clean and divot shots (20 balls); and then with your 10 wood, alternating full-swing divot and clean shots through another 20 balls. The purpose of this warm up is not only to stretch and heat your golfing muscles, but also to enable you to regroove your basic woodiron swing after a night's rest.

Before you play any round of golf, you should always warm up this way at the practice tee, starting with your 15 wood until you are hitting full-swing shots with it, then working down through the rest of your clubs, stroking two or three balls with each. Concentrate as you go on the fundamentals of grip, stance, address, and swing. By the time you are ready to tee off, not only will you be loose, but all the physical components of your swing will be well locked into your muscle memory. Any golfer who fails to warm up properly before a round has only himself to blame for his poor performance.

Once you've thoroughly warmed up with the 15 and 10 woods, you are ready to proceed to your first 5-wood drill of the morning.

SECOND DRILL

Put 5 balls down on the tee; then address and hit each as you are accustomed to doing with your 5 wood. After you've finished, forget the distance and direction of each shot. Instead, analyze your swing. Was it perceptibly *different* from the swing you've gotten used to with the 15 and 10 wood? The chances are good that it was. Yes, you stood farther away from the ball and your swing arc was longer, but that's only natural because of the longer length of the 5 wood's shaft. But within these parameters your swing still felt different. Why?

Most golfers of average ability tend to swing the 5 wood to strike the ball in a swooping, scooping manner. They look at the inviting loft angle of the club face and automatically think: "Aha, this club is meant to get the ball into the air, so I'll help it along with my arms and hands."

Wrong. This is the reason so many golfers top or hit their 5 woods, and other fairway woods, offline so often. Again, they refuse to let the club face do the work.

The proper swing with the 5 wood is no different in its basic properties from the swing you've learned with the 10 and 15 woods. The ball should be played forward of the midline of your body but not too far forward—not, for instance, off the toe of your leading foot. Indeed, although you will stand farther away from the ball with the 5 wood, it should be in the same position, in relation to your feet, as it is when you play full shots with the 10 and 15 wood.

The swing itself is also executed as with a high-numbered wood. In other words, you want to strike the ball directly with the club face at the bottom of your swing arc, but while the club head is still moving downward and an instant before it starts its upward arc leading to the follow-through. Your follow-through should always, of course, carry your arms, hands, and club high and forward so that they are all facing the target—a basic rule of any golf swing. This helps ensure that you have hit the ball with the club face pointing straight ahead rather than at a hook or slice angle.

Repeat: Strike the ball directly with the club face just before your swing arc reaches its bottom-most point and starts upward. Do not try to hit it at the beginning of the upward arc—a "scooping" action. And do not try to brush the grass directly to the rear of the ball as you hit it—a "swooping" action. These swing techniques will frequently get the ball up and away, but just as frequently they will result in mis-hits.

Now, put down a row of 20 balls and, applying these principles, set yourself up to each with your 5 wood and hit it. Concentrate intently on your basic woodiron swing mechanics—tempo, pace, rhythm, balance, weight transfer between backswing and follow-through—and swing easily. Then analyze what happened with these 20 shots.

It is likely that they felt and looked quite different from what you're accustomed to with the 5 wood, just as the slightly different swing—controlled as opposed to full power—felt awkward. And your balls will not have gone as far as you're used to seeing them go when you hit a good bashing 5-wood shot—maybe 20 or 30 yards less. Don't worry about it, for you will be working back up to those more generous distances as you become more comfortable with the changed swing.

The point of your analysis should be to discover what you are still doing wrong. Did you hit every ball directly at the bottom of your swing? Did you follow through high? Did your weight transfer and body turn feel comfortable? Have you found the right stance and address? Have you adjusted your grip until you've found the one that produces the straightest shots? Did you swing "within yourself" on each shot? Did you stay down on each? (Staying down almost guarantees that you'll strike the ball correctly at the very bottom of your swing arc.)

After you've sorted out what you did right and what you did wrong, hit another 20 balls with your focus on improving your swing and ball-striking performance. Now you'll start to get the hang of the proper 5-wood shot.

Hit yet another 20 balls. This time gradually increase the pace, force, and tempo of your swing without letting it get out of hand. Now your shots will begin to carry the distances you like to see, bulleting away from the tee straight and in a medium high arc. For a clearer visual idea of the loft-distance factor you want to get out of your 5 wood, consult the comparative trajectory drawing of these factors for the 5 wood, the 10 wood, and the 15 wood. It is based on an average 15-wood distance factor of 110 yards. (See Fig. 56.)

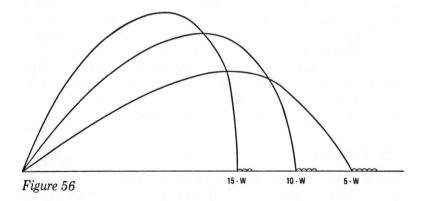

Figure 56

THIRD DRILL

Measure the average distance of your last ten 5-wood shots and set up a target at that distance out on the range. (Your average distance by now should be 20 to 40 yards farther than your 10-wood distance factor of yesterday.) Then go back to the practice tee and hit twenty 5-wood shots at the target. Concentrate on maintaining your proper swing mechanics, but apply a bit more force with each shot until you reach the borderline between swinging *in control* and swinging *out of control.* This borderline will be your maximum 5-wood swing force and swing tempo; you will quickly learn to recognize it.

Now hit another 20 balls at a swing tempo and force that is just under the maximum you have established. This we'll call your "ideal" swing force and tempo. It is this you now must groove.

Hit 40 more balls, concentrating on striking each ball with your ideal force-tempo factor. When you've finished, pace off your average distance once again. When you've calculated your new average distance, which should be 40 to 60 yards above your 10-wood maximum distance factor, you will have found your maximum distance-factor for the 5 wood. Now you are ready to start fine-tuning your 5-wood stroke.

FOURTH DRILL

Reset your target at your final maximum distance factor for the 5 wood. Hit 20 balls at the target, using your ideal force-tempo swing. The results will confirm the distance you are capable of getting out of the 5 wood when you use it as a long woodiron.

Now stroke another 20 shots, this time hitting for accuracy as well as distance. Keep hitting until you can put at least half your shots within 20 yards of your target. When you can do this, you are well on your way to becoming a proficient 5-wood player.

FIFTH DRILL

For this, your next-to-last drill of the morning, hit 20 balls as though you were using the 5 wood as a driver. Tee each ball up, but very low so that the bottom of the ball remains in contact with the grass. You will be using the 5 wood for tee shots on certain par-3 holes equivalent in distance to your maximum distance factor with the club—holes of 160 yards, 180 yards, 200 yards in length, depending on your natural power.

The swing and swing mechanics remain the same: stay down on the ball and hit through it so that the club face strikes the ball an instant before it reaches the bottom of the swing arc. Such teed-up shots should give you the same distance and accuracy as shots off the turf, but with a few yards more loft so that the ball won't roll as far when it lands—an important aspect of 5-wood play when you are hitting to a well-guarded green on a long par-3 hole.

Keep hitting these tee shots until you consistently obtain the higher loft while still achieving your maximum 5-wood distance. Don't forget to continue to groove your swing as you stroke each ball.

SIXTH DRILL

Finish up the morning session by going out on your course and finding, if possible, a par-3 hole that is roughly equivalent (give or take 10 yards) in distance to the maximum distance factor you've established for your 5 wood. Hit 40 tee shots to the green to see how you do. If you get at least half the balls on the green, as I think you will, your transition to the Woodiron Method is nicely on schedule.

13

The fourth day: afternoon session

You can't complain that you've had to give up playing golf during your training and transition period. This afternoon you will play yet another 18 holes. This time you will add your 5 wood to your 10 wood, 15 wood, and putter. And, like yesterday, you will keep score.

Now that you are going to add a 5 wood to your still limited club arsenal, you will have an excellent chance of improving on the score you made yesterday with just your 10 and 15 woods to get you from tee to green. To see what I mean, look again at the first hole of the Links. As you followed me over this 390-yard par-4 hole yesterday and the day before, when I was using my 15 wood and then my 10 wood added to it, you saw that on each occasion it took me three shots to reach the green. Let's play it again on paper, but this time with the 5 wood added to my limited club repertoire. Indeed, just before sitting down to write this chapter, I played an 18-hole round over the Links with just a 5 wood, 10 wood, 15 wood, and putter. Here is how I fared on the now familiar first hole.

I drove off the first tee with my 5 wood—a regular, slightly teed-up drive. My maximum distance factor with the 5 wood over a level piece of ground is 200 yards, and that's almost exactly what I got from my straight tee shot. This left me with a 190-yard downhill second shot to the middle of the open-fronted first green. If I used a full 5 wood for my second shot, I figured, and hit it straight, I would hit the back of the green, probably, and go into, or over, the rear trap (the downhill aspect of the shot added 10 to 15 yards to my 5-wood distance factor). At 190 yards from where I was to the center of the green, if I hit my 10 wood, which would only get me 170 yards in the air with the downhill factor, I would end up landing the ball short of the green. But with the downhill slant of the fairway in front of the green, I could reasonably assume that my shot, if I hit it straight, would bounce and roll onto the foreportion of the putting surface.

I chose the 10-wood shot and got the desired result, my ball rolling to a stop 5 feet onto the green and 20 feet from the pin. Two putts gave me a par-4 score on the hole. True, I had a 4 the last time I played the hole. But this was an easier 4 because I managed to get onto the green in two strokes and didn't have to rely on making a one-putt.

The real difference the 5 wood made in my score for the entire round over the Links first showed up on the 420-yard par-4 fourth hole. You'll recall that last time out I scored a 6 on this hole, primarily because I tried to force a 10-wood shot into traveling farther than my maximum distance-factor for that club. This time, a 200-yard 5-wood tee shot and a full 10-wood second shot enabled me to lay up in front of the narrow fairway trap 40 yards in front of the forward edge of the green. My third shot was a half-choke, three-quarter-swing pitch that I landed at the front edge of the green and ran up to within 4 feet of the pin. I made the putt for a score of par 4 this time, instead of my previous double-bogey 6.

My whole round was proportionately better. For instance, on the 500-yard par-5 seventh I scored a bogey 6 last time without a 5 wood. This time, my first two shots with my 5 wood left me 110 yards short of the green and 20 yards in front of the pond (see map). A nice three-quarter-swing 15-wood pitch put me 25 feet from the pin on my third shot. I two-putted for a par 5.

And then there were the 450-yard par-5 thirteenth hole, the 190-yard par-3 fifteenth, and the 480-yard par-5 seventeenth. With the addition of my 5 wood, I cut a stroke off my scores on each of these holes. For the entire 18 holes I came in with a score of 80, 3 lower than my previous round and a mere 8 over par for the course! The reason I wasn't even lower was because I was not as lucky with my putting as before. But from tee to green I registered a significant improvement. (I only had to make three shots from sand traps.)

Again I've taken you partly around the Links on paper, this time with a 5 wood. I've done so in order to impress on you the fact that the time has come to "premanage" your own coming 5-wood practice round. By that I mean that you should, before starting this afternoon's round, draw a map of your own course similar in detail to the map of the Links. Put in every trap and water hazard, every yardage per hole, every fairway bend, every rise and fall of ground. Then study each hole before you go out to play your practice round. Plan each shot—a 5 wood here, a 10 wood there; a 15-wood cut chip if here, a 15-wood full-swing pitch if there; and so on. In other words, preplay your round on paper before you go out and actually play it.

By doing this, you will prepare yourself much better than you might otherwise for a maximum-benefit practice round with your three woodirons. Don't be surprised if you come in with the lowest score of your life—particularly if you are a golfer whose handicap has never been lower than 15.

The fifth day:
morning session

Now that you have become acquainted with the three basic clubs of the Woodiron Method, it is time to expand your repertoire. To do that, you should add an 8 wood and a 12 wood to the three woodirons you have already. You will spend this morning acclimating yourself to these two new clubs.

The 8 wood is the equivalent of the 4 iron, and the 12 wood is the equivalent of the 8 iron. In effect, what you have in your woodiron arsenal now is a 1 iron, a 4 iron, a 6 iron, an 8 iron, and a combination sand-and-pitching wedge. Add to these your putter, your driver, and a long fairway wood such as a 3 or 4, and you have all you need, basically, to play much more effective golf. Certainly as you improve and work to refine your game more, you can add further woodirons until you reach your maximum allowable club quantity of fourteen. But I think you'll agree that at this point you don't need fourteen clubs to play much better golf than you're accustomed to playing. You've already proved that by your past two woodiron practice rounds, when you most likely scored significantly better with just two or three woodiron clubs and a putter than you ever have with a full bag of conventional woods and irons.

Before you start your drills with the 8 and 12 woods, you

should figure out the approximate yardage you can expect from them. Simply add 16 yards to the distance factor you have established for your 10 wood to arrive at your likely 8-wood distance factor; and subtract 16 yards from the 10-wood factor to get the factor you can expect from the 12 wood. In other words, if your 10-wood distance factor is about 140 yards, you can figure on hitting the 8 wood consistently about 156 yards and the 12 wood about 124 yards. This represents a differential of 32 yards.

Now, go out on the range and set up targets at the respective distances you've calculated for the 8 and 12 woods—the second 32 yards farther away from the tee than the first. Then, on your way back to the tee, drop a third target at a spot, closer in, that is equivalent to your 15 wood's maximum distance factor.

FIRST DRILL

This is a warm-up drill with your 15 wood. Hit 20 balls, starting with short shots and working up to shots aimed at your closest target. Concentrate on swing form and technique until you are sure you are in the right groove. Stroke another 20 balls, working on coming as close to your nearest target as you can with each 15-wood shot.

SECOND DRILL

Now start hitting with your newly acquired 12 wood. Except for the fact that the 12 wood's shaft is a little longer than the 15 wood's and you will therefore set up a little farther away from the ball, everything about the 12-wood stroke is the same as that of the 15 wood. Hit your first 20 balls "soft"—that is, without your full woodiron swing force. Simply endeavor to make the club face come into clean, crisp contact with the ball and execute a good follow-through. This will give you a clear mental image of, and muscle-memory feel for, the manner in which the 12 wood does the work.

With your next 20 balls, begin to exert increasing swing force until your force and tempo are at their maximum while still under control. With these shots you will start to loft the ball over a distance of ground that is roughly equivalent to the distance factor you have calculated for the 12 wood. Your shots, although perhaps not always straight, should carry beyond your 15-wood target and land near a line drawn laterally through the second target. Once you achieve this distance consistently, you can start to narrow in on the target.

Hit another 20 to 40 balls—all full-swing clean shots—at your 12-wood target. If the first few go consistently long or consistently short when you swing with optimum force and tempo, go out and adjust your target to the overage or underage you are getting. If some go short while others go long, however, leave the target as is and concentrate on refining your swing tempo and force until you come close to the mark with each shot.

THIRD DRILL

Switch now to 20 divot shots, executing them just as you've learned to do with the 10 and 15 woods. Concentrate on shallow divots after striking the ball and full follow-throughs. Your shots should carry 10 to 20 yards less distance than your clean shots, but they should soar on a higher arc. Indeed, they should land closer to your 15-wood target than your 12-wood marker.

FOURTH DRILL

Now hit 40 more balls, alternating divot shots with clean ones and trying to achieve a further consistency of distance with each. Here you are learning more about the concept of using various woodirons for shots in various situations. For instance, suppose your 15-wood maximum distance factor over level ground is 110 yards, your maximum clean-shot distance factor with the 12 wood is 130 yards, and your 12-wood divot shot distance factor is 120 yards. And suppose you are faced with an approach shot of 120 yards to the center of a green guarded in front and rear by large traps or other hazards. A full, clean 15-wood pitch shot will probably carry short into the front trap, while a full, clean 12-wood shot will carry too far. What you want in this situation is a full 12-wood divot shot—your best guarantee of achieving the right distance and stopping power.

Let us add to the foregoing mix a stiff following wind. The wind lengthens your 15-wood distance factor by 10 to 15 yards. Hence, you would make the clean 15-wood shot instead of the 12-wood divot shot. Under the constantly varying weather and course conditions of an actual round of golf, once you have mastered your expanding array of woodirons, you will begin to choose specific clubs for the special conditions surrounding each shot; you will not go by distance factor alone.

FIFTH DRILL

Exchange the 8 wood for the 12 wood. With it, repeat each of the three previous drills in order, working up to making full clean shots to your most distant target. Adjust the target's distance if necessary after you've settled on a comfortable maximum distance factor. Then switch over to divot shots. Finally, alternate divot shots with clean ones.

SIXTH DRILL

By now you should be thoroughly comfortable with both the 8 and 12 woods and be able to get reasonably good results from each club. For this drill, then, hit about 40 balls, alternating between the 8 wood and the 12 wood, and alternating too between clean and divot shots with each. Concentrate with each shot on coming as close as you can to the respective targets you've set out for the two clubs.

SEVENTH DRILL

Find a par-3 hole on your golf course that is roughly equivalent in distance to the maximum distance factor you've established for your 12 wood. If you can't find a par-3 short enough, then locate a hole equivalent in distance to your 8-wood distance factor. Best of all, find two par-3 holes, each of which is roughly equivalent to your distance factor for each club.

The idea is to practice 40 tee shots to the respective greens with each club. If the shortest par 3 on your course is 140 yards and your 12-wood distance factor is, say, only 125 yards, then use your

10 wood instead. If your 8-wood clean-shot distance factor is 155 yards, say, and the closest par-3 hole is only 140 yards, alternate your practice tee shots between 8-wood divot shots and 10-wood clean shots to determine which give you the best results at that distance. Keep practicing, whether on one or two par 3s, until you get half these tee shots on the green.

EIGHTH DRILL

Still at the par-3 holes you have selected, use your 15 wood as a follow-up to get onto the green and as close to the pin as possible all those balls that fell short, wide, or far when you hit your practice tee shots. Use the full range of long and short chips—straight and cut—sandblasts and short pitches you have learned with your 15 wood. Deal with each recovery shot deliberately and seriously. Select the best technique (half-choke; three-quarter-swing cut shot; putting-style straight chip; and so on) for each, and play each shot as though it were an *actual shot* needed to save par. Of course, you won't feel the same kind of pressure you'd feel if you were playing each shot in an actual round of competitive golf. But the drill, if you go at it intently, will take you a long way toward further refining and expanding your skills with the 15 wood in an almost infinite variety of close-to-the-green trouble situations.

15

The fifth day: afternoon session

This afternoon you will play another round of golf—in the same fashion you played yesterday's, but with your new 8 wood and 12 wood added to your 5, 10, and 15 woods and putter. Before you start out, though, remember to do two things. First, study the map you have made of your course and preplay your round on paper, plotting where you would like each shot to go and imagining what woodiron you would use in any given position. Second, warm up with 40 balls off the practice tee, starting with ten mixed divot and clean 15-wood shots, 5 shots each with your 12, 10, 8, and 5 woods and finishing with 10 short alternating cut and straight 15-wood chip shots. Then go to the practice green and stroke 10 or so short running chips to a cup. Finish up with a few minutes of putting practice.

As you play this afternoon's round, you will use the 5 wood on all holes that call for the longest shots you can produce. You will use your higher-numbered woods for the approach shots that are most appropriate to each. Although you will be trying to beat your improved score of yesterday, the likelihood is that you won't do as well today unless you *really* concentrate on each shot. This is because the addition of the 8 and 12 woods will complicate your club selection for any given shot. Rather than ease matters for you, the wider club option will actually make things more difficult at first. Your tendency, if you are like most converts to woodirons, will be to try to get a little more distance than your distance factor for a given club allows. This means that you will force several of your shots and end up in needless trouble.

Actually it is not a bad idea to yield to such temptations during this round, for it will serve as a vital object lesson. As you proceed through the round, you will learn firsthand that there is a woodiron for every shot you will ever need to make. Today, it is only a matter of fact that you don't yet have all the necessary clubs; you will be tempted to try to compensate for that by forcing an occasional long shot that you would be able to make easily with one or two clubs lower in number—clubs you don't yet have in your bag.

By the time you get halfway through the round, however, you should realize what you're doing and see the light. Go back to letting the few clubs you *do* have with you do the work. Soon enough you will have all the clubs you need to make the shots you can't quite make today.

Again, before you go out for today's round, it might be instructive to play a few holes on paper with me over my course—the Links—in order to get a clearer idea of what you should and shouldn't do on your round. Since I've taken you over the Links' front 9 before, let's see how I negotiated the back 9 using only the clubs that you will be using today.

Tenth Hole: Par 4: 400 yards. This straight hole undulates gradually downhill to a medium-sized green flanked by a deep bunker on the left and a large pot bunker at the right forefront (see map). That which is not bunkered around the sides and rear of the green is a long, steep and stubbly fall-off that invariably means trouble for anyone who overshoots the green.

My tee shot was with my 5 wood. It flew straight and came to rest 200 yards out and 200 yards from the center of the green. A second shot downhill with the 5 wood might carry me over the green, I figured, so I used my 8 wood for my approach. A clean stroke lofted my ball 170 yards downhill so that it hit just in front of the green. Even at that, it rolled to a stop at left rear, about 26 feet from the pin. Two putts gave me a *score of par 4.*

Eleventh Hole: Par 3: 180 yards. This is a fairly long par 3 made even longer by the fact that one must drive uphill over the wide gorge to an elevated, well-trapped green. Its redeeming factor is that one doesn't have to land one's tee shot directly on the putting surface, but can bounce the ball up after clearing the fairway trap in front, which is 150 yards from the tee.

I used my 5 wood off the tee and, although I hit it straight, didn't quite reach the green. However, with my 15 wood, I stroked a nice 50-foot straight chip to within 3 feet of the cup on my second shot. I holed out in one putt for a *score of par 3.*

Twelfth Hole: Par 4: 420 yards. I've seldom been able to reach the green in regulation on this sharply uphill 420-yarder, even with a driver and a 3-wood second shot. I therefore planned only to get on in three, starting with my 5-wood shot from the tee across the gorge. My tee shot put me out 175 yards in the right center of the fairway. My second shot with the same club got me another 170 yards uphill, leaving me with an uphill approach to the side-trapped green of 70 yards, or an actual distance of about 90 yards. For my third shot I hit a full-swing half-choke 15 wood. The ball, unfortunately, hit a few feet short of the green and just trickled on, stopping 50 feet from the cup. Misreading my first putt, I left it a good eight feet short and needed two more strokes to get down in a *2 over par 6.*

Thirteenth Hole: Par 5: 460 yards. A look at the map will show you that this slight dogleg to the right demands a tee shot over a pond into the fairway. A huge trap yawns on the right side of the fairway to catch sliced or faded drives of between 180 and 220 yards in length. My 180-yard 5-wood drive faded over the pond. Although it didn't get into the trap itself, it stopped in the high grass just in front of it.

The lie wasn't very good, so instead of hitting the 5 wood for my second shot, I hit my 8 wood. The ball came out nicely and traveled 160 yards to the middle of the fairway.

My third shot was a 120-yarder. But because the fairway rose to the elevated, open-fronted green, it was more like 140 yards. My distance factor with my 12 wood is about 140 yards, but I decided to go to my 10 wood and hit a divot shot, which would also give me about 140 yards. I hit a classic-looking shot; the ball soared straight at the pin and stopped 20 feet beyond. Two putts put me down in *par 5.*

Fourteenth Hole: Par 4: 290 yards. This a short par 4. But it is not easy, due to the traps encircling the small green; to get on in regulation demands a precision second shot even after a long, straight tee shot with a driver. I had no driver, so I hit a 5-wood tee shot 180 yards out onto the uprising fairway. This left me with a 110-yard second approach shot that required me to loft the ball over the front trap. I used my 12 wood and hit a divot shot. Going uphill still, my ball just got over the front trap and stopped 20 feet from the pin. Two putts got me home in a *score of par 4.*

Fifteenth Hole: Par 3: 190 yards. This is a downhill par 3 that I can reach with a well-hit, straight 5 wood, although I often tend to run the ball over the green and into the rear trap with this club because of the downhill factor. I therefore used my 8 wood off the tee. I barely cleared the front fairway trap and came to rest four yards from the front of the green. A straight 15-wood running chip put me 3 feet from the cup, and a single putt got me down for a *score of par 3.*

On the slightly downhill sixteenth hole, 400 yards long, I got on the green in 3 and made a bogey 5 with two putts.

On the gradually uphill seventeenth, a 500-yard par 5, I made a good 5-wood tee shot but put my second shot, also a 5 wood, into the big trap on the right, at the bend of the fairway. From the trap I was 130 yards from the green. I hit my 10 wood out of the sand at the green and got a little too much on it: my ball ended up in the medium-deep trap at the back of the green. I let my concentration lapse trying to blast out of the trap on my next shot. As a result, it took me two strokes to get out of the trap and onto the green with my 15 wood. Two putts gave me a *double-bogey 7*.

On the eighteenth hole—downhill from the tee, then uphill over a brook to the green—I pulled my 5-wood tee shot into the left-hand fairway trap, leaving myself no chance of getting near the green on my second shot. I used my 8 wood out of the trap to lay up in front of the brook, which was 80 yards from the center of the narrow, kidney-shaped green. For my third shot, steeply uphill, I played a full-grip, three-quarter-swing 15 wood and landed the ball on the putting surface, 25 feet from the cup. Two putts gave me a *score of bogey 5*.

For the back nine, then, I had a total score of 42 as against par for the nine of 36. I had made a 43 on the front nine, so my total for the round was 85. Not bad, but not great. Yet much better, again, than I was accustomed to scoring when playing with a full set of conventional irons.

You too can enjoy such breakthrough success if you apply all your concentration to each shot and make sure not to try to get more distance out of any particular club you choose than you are capable of with your grooved woodiron swing. Remember also that today's round is first and foremost a learning experience. Hence, don't allow yourself to get discouraged by the occasional misplayed shot. Analyze what you did wrong and correct it with your next shot.

Finally, when you are confronted with the choice of making a safe shot or a high-risk shot that is likely to put you into trouble, always go for the safe shot. You are still learning the woodirons, and you are not yet ready to start becoming "aggressive" with them. Later on, when you've gotten fully proficient with them, you can start to gamble a bit.

16

The sixth day: morning session

Now you are ready to put back into your game some of the distance you've been lacking during the past few days. You will do this, of course, with your driver (or whatever other wood you usually use for par-4 and par-5 tee shots) and your regular fairway woods. The only difference is that you will tame these clubs down a bit as you apply the principles of your basic woodiron swing to them. With the confidence you are acquiring in your woodirons, your tendency to blast every long tee and fairway wood shot as far as you can will be tempered. You have learned already that you don't need super-long tee shots to improve your golf game. On the contrary, the importance of distance pales in comparison to driving and fairway wood accuracy when you've got your trusty woodirons to get you to the green.

The purpose of most of this morning's session is to teach you, or enable you to teach yourself, to adapt your driving and long-wood game to your woodiron game. This means that having learned what you have about the potential of woodirons markedly to improve your game, you must commit yourself to trading driving and fairway wood distance for accuracy.

If you have discovered your natural distance factor with your 8 wood to be, say, 180 yards, then you are a powerful golfer who is probably capable of driving the ball 240 to 250 yards on those occasions when you manage to hit it straight off the tee. If your 8-wood distance factor is, say, 160 yards, then your distance potential on a straight drive is probably 210 to 220 yards. If your 8-wood distance factor is only 140 yards, then your maximum distance off the tee is probably 180 to 190 yards.

Whatever your maximum distance potential is with your driver or other driving wood, I want you to forget it for now. Put it out of mind. Renounce it. When you play woodiron golf, you will no longer need to try to hit every drive or fairway wood as far as you can. Instead, you will hit well short of your potential (20 to 40 yards less), at least at the beginning, and concentrate on placing your drives and long wood shots so that they best set up the most important shots of your game—your woodiron approach shots to the green.

Look once again at the layout of the first hole on the Links map. It is 390 yards long—a relatively easy par 4 for the accurate, less than long distance golfer, a relatively hard par 4 for the long but inaccurate player. Let's suppose that you are capable of driving 240 yards when you let out all the stops, but that only one out of every five such drives goes straight. On that one drive at the Links' first hole, you will be left with a 150-yard downhill approach to the open-fronted green from a nice fairway lie. The other four drives might land in the driving traps on either side of the fairway, or in the rough or trees beyond, leaving you with longer approach shots from inferior lies and with the greenside traps between you and the pin. Whereas you have a good chance to get on the green with your 150-yard approach from the fairway, your chances are practically nil with your other four shots.

Now, imagine taking 20 yards out of your driving swing, modulating its force, energy, and tempo so that four out of your five drives go straight but only 220 yards. Now you're faced with four clean and open approaches to the green instead of one. The fact that they are 170 yards long instead of 150 yards is not really significant. If you can hit, say, your 10 wood with confidence and accuracy to the green from 150 yards, you can do the same with your 7 or 8 wood from 170 yards out.

What you have done with your shorter, more accurate drives is to improve your chances of getting on the green in regulation, and therefore scoring a par, by 60 per cent. Instead of being in a position to reach the green safely one out of five times you now are in a position to do so four out of five times. What a controlled driver or fairway wood does for you is to keep you out of trouble and set up your woodiron approach shots to the green most effectively. Every par 4 golf hole starts with your tee shot. But as you get ready to tee off, you should be thinking of where you want to be when you are ready to make the hole's most vital shot—the approach to the green.

The same principle applies to the longer par-5 holes. Take a look at the Links' longest par 5, the 500-yard seventh hole. A maximum-length but wild drive of 240 yards will either sail into the trees on the left or bounce down the steep bank of high rough on the right of the fairway. Thus your second shot is already a trouble shot, and your chances of reaching the green in regulation are drastically reduced.

Now picture a drive of only 220 yards in distance but fairly straight. If you manage to avoid the driving trap on the right, you are set up for a simple second fairway shot that will in turn set up an easy third approach to the green. If you can get 220 straight yards consistently with your driver, you should be able to get 180 to 200 straight yards with a controlled-swing fairway wood shot for your second stroke, leaving you nicely located in front of the pond for a simple 80 to 100 yard pitch approach with your 15 wood.

On this hole, even if you managed to blast a mighty and straight 240-yard drive, you would still be forced to lay up in front of the pond on your second shot unless you were strong enough to carry the water with your 3 wood (a shot requiring at least 225 yards in the air). So an all-out booming drive from the seventh tee is a waste of energy and daring. The more prudent tee shot is a shorter drive with much greater accuracy.

Look over the rest of the par-4 and par-5 holes on the Links and see where the most effective "controlled-driving" targets lie. They are marked on the map by the circled x symbols, which represent a distance of 200 to 220 yards from each tee. Then go over the map of your own course and insert similar symbols at the equivalent yardages. These are your optimum tee-shot targets. Of course, if you do not have the strength and timing to drive at least 200 yards with a controlled swing, move your personal target areas back toward each tee accordingly. The loss of distance, as you've already seen, won't hurt your game in any significant way (maybe three strokes per round) as long as you play with optimum accuracy.

Now for this morning's drills, which are designed to revamp your driving and long wood game into a consistently accurate one.

FIRST DRILL

First, go through a thorough warm-up at the practice tee with your five woodirons, working down from the 15 wood to the 5 wood. Then hit 10 teed-up balls with your driver, swinging at them as hard as you can. Make note of how many of your drives go reasonably straight and how many veer or curve offline. If more than half go reasonably straight, you are in a good position to adapt faster to the complete woodiron game than if more than half go offline.

Now, continue to hit more drives in sets of 10 balls each, slightly reducing the force and effort of your swing with each set until you arrive at a set in which 8 of your 10 shots go straight—albeit for shorter distances than you're used to.

Finally, hit another set of 20 drives, fine-tuning your swing force and tempo in accordance with the last set. If 17 of your 20 shots go straight, you have found your proper driving swing. Now, hit another 10 balls and make a conscious effort to send every drive straight. Keep working on your modulated swing until you can hit 10 reasonably straight drives in a row.

SECOND DRILL

Measure the average distance of your last 10 straight drives. Then go onto your golf course with 20 balls and find a level par-4 hole that no one will be playing for at least 20 minutes. Set up a target in the center of the fairway at a distance from the tee of the average yardage you have calculated. Go back to the tee and hit 20 drives, trying with each to come as close to the target as you can.

Standing on a real tee looking down a real fairway to a distant green will tend to create a different psychology from that of the practice range. Suddenly visual pressures will intrude to tighten you up—the narrowness of the fairway, distant traps, perhaps a hazard that you have to drive over on your tee shot, plus the natural urge always to drive as far as you can.

This drill is designed to help you discipline yourself against such pressures and urges. You will probably force many of your first 20 tee shots and hit them far but wild. So collect your balls, go back to the tee, and hit them again—this time completely forgetting about getting maximum distance and focusing solely on placing your drives close to your target area.

Keep working at this drill until you can put 18 out of every 20 drives in your general fairway target area. Then find a par-5 tee and repeat the routine.

THIRD DRILL

Return to the practice range and repeat the first drill, this time with your 3 wood or 4 wood—whichever one you usually prefer for long second shots. Now, of course, you must hit off the turf rather than from tees. Continue working at the fairway wood until you can hit 10 consecutive shots straight and for a distance that falls roughly between the distance factors of your driver and 5 wood, respectively.

FOURTH DRILL

Now go to a par-5 or extra long par-4 hole on your course. Establish yourself on the fairway at a point that is the same distance away from the tee as your accurate driving distance. Shooting in the direction of the green, hit 20 fairway wood shots, concentrating on accuracy and setting yourself up for the most advantageous third shots to the green. Once you've achieved a consistent distance and direction, continue to refine your shots until you feel confident that you can hit any fairway wood in the vicinity of where you want it to go.

FIFTH DRILL

Find a spot anywhere on your course from which you have to hit your fairway woods from a fairly steep uphill lie. Hit 20 balls toward the green from here, adjusting your stance and address until you find the right combination you need to make the best and most consistent shots. Repeat the drill from a fairly steep downhill lie.

Run through the drill again from sidehill lies—one where the ball is on a higher level than your feet, the other where it is lower. On the higher-level shots, stand farther away from the ball than normal; on the lower, set up closer to the ball. Work on each of these shots until you can hit most of your balls consistently straight and over the distance you've established as most comfortable for your basic fairway wood.

SIXTH DRILL

Take your driving club, basic fairway wood, 10 wood, and 15 wood out to the first par-4 hole on your course. Playing only one ball, drive it in accordance with what you've learned about par-4 tee shots. If you end up at a distance from the green that is less than your basic fairway wood distance factor, use the appropriate woodiron for your second shot to the green. If your drive leaves you far enough away from the green so that you cannot even reach it with your 3 or 4 wood, try to place your second shot with one of these woods directly in front of the green, setting yourself up for an easy woodiron chip or pitch to the pin.

Repeat this drill over several further par-4 holes. Then go through it again on a couple of par-5s—once more concentrating on placing your drive and second shot consecutively so as to set up the easiest shot to the green with one of your woodirons.

The sixth day:
afternoon session

You have by now essentially revamped your entire tee-to-green game. And you are at a point where you have the potential to start playing regularly at scores that are half your present handicap, or less. If you are a 28-handicapper who usually shoots 100 over a par-72 course, you should now be able to score around 86 consistently. If you are a 20-handicapper who generally shoots 92, you should be able to score around 82 with regularity. And if you are a 12-handicapper who shoots 84, you should be able to score around 78.

But this potential is still on paper. How soon you actually reach it depends on how quickly and efficiently you can put all the woodiron principles you've learned into practice, and how well you are able to sustain them time and again during your future golf rounds.

This afternoon you are going to test your progress in these two departments for the first time with a full, if limited, range of woods and woodirons. The test is in the form of another round over your course, this time adding your driver and basic fairway wood to your 5, 8, 10, 12, and 15-wood collection.

Before you start, carry out the following three procedures. First, preplay the entire round on paper, using the detailed map you have made of your course to plot your approach to each hole. Decide where you want to put each tee shot in accordance with the reduced-distance but increased-accuracy principles you worked on this morning. From there, calculate your probable distances from each green and, taking into account the trouble you will need to get over or avoid, make a realistic decision about the proper club to use for your second shot in any given situation. Keep in mind as you do this that you are committed to using the right club for the distance involved and other conditions such as lie and wind. (Remember, a clean shot hit from a downhill lie will produce considerably more distance than a shot from an uphill lie. So, where your 12 wood might be sufficient from a downhill lie, you will need to move down to your 10 wood or even 8 wood from a steeply uphill lie.) Take all these factors into consideration as you plan your woodiron approach-to-the-green shots, again determining realistically the proper club and shot to use to get you on the green in no more than one shot over regulation for that hole. (With the woodirons, any time you have to take an extra shot over regulation to get on the green, you should intend the shot to get you close enough to the pin for a one-putt to save par for the hole.) Finally, carefully plot your play of the par-3 holes with a view to getting on the greens every time with your tee shots.

Second, go through a thorough warm-up with all your clubs on the practice tee before starting out, concentrating on grooving your swing tempo and swing force with each club. Then go to the practice green and run through short and long straight chips and cut chips with your 15 wood until you have a good feel for these shots. Finish up with some putting practice. (If there is a practice sand trap handy, hit a few shots out of that as well.)

Now comes perhaps your most important preround warm-up ritual. Basically it is a mental routine designed to focus your concentration, resolve, and self-discipline toward carrying out properly all the principles of the woodiron game. When I first switched to woodirons, I wrote the following words on the back of my hand to aid me in this:

1. Tempo
2. Follow thru
3. Confidence

I used these as code words to prepare myself mentally for each round. They told me to keep my swing in control on each shot, to follow through completely, and to approach each shot with confidence rather than doubt or trepidation. Later I reduced the words to an acronym: TEFOLCO. This symbolized the basic tenets of my new woodiron game and served to keep me focused on them at all times on the golf course: to let each club do its work; to refrain from forcing any shot or trying to get more distance than a given club will faithfully produce when swung with proper tempo and force; and to use each shot most effectively to set up the next one.

There are the basic principles of the woodiron game that you should run over in your mind again and again as you prepare to tee off on this or any future round of golf. As soon as you set up for your first drive, you will feel all your old urges and instincts to blast away at the ball return. You must resist them on your first shot and on all subsequent shots, and substitute in their place a calm, deliberate, and confident approach.

The quicker you are able to do this, to make it a matter of second nature so that it sustains you over an entire round, the faster you will begin to exploit the full potential of the Woodiron Method to reduce your handicap sharply.

18

The seventh day: morning session

The Bible says that God created the world in six days and, on the seventh, rested. On this the seventh day of the "re-creation" of your golf game, you are not going to rest. You are going to pause, however, to analyze and reassess.

The first thing you should analyze is your practice round of yesterday afternoon. Yes, you made some mistakes, occasionally gave into old urges, and even simply misplayed or mis-hit a few shots. This is not unusual. The important thing is that, if you are like nine out of every ten mid- to high-handicap golfers who have switched to woodirons following the schedule I have outlined in the preceding pages, you scored *at least* six strokes below your present handicap. And some of you even made scores that represented a true halving of your handicap.

All things considered, you should be pleased with yesterday's round despite the fact that you did a few things not so pleasing. Go back to the map of your course and try to isolate those situations in which you failed to hit the wood or woodiron shot you'd intended. Consider what you did wrong. More likely than not it was a matter of not having enough confidence in the woodiron you used, or of being fooled or confused by the distance of the shot.

157

If such were the case, the time has come to consider rounding out your woodiron collection. For instance, the first time I played a practice round over the Links with my driver, 3 wood, and a limited selection of woodirons, I ran into similar club-confusion trouble on the third hole. With two pars behind me, I was feeling really good as I prepared to drive from the third tee. I put my drive almost exactly where I wanted it to go—225 yards out in the fairway between the two traps. This left me with a second shot to the green of 185 yards, but it meant that I would have to carry the trap that sits in the fairway 10 yards in front of the green. Although it looked farther away, I figured the far edge of that trap to be 165 yards from where my ball rested. I debated overlong about whether to use my 10 wood, whose distance factor was about 165 yards, and try just to clear the trap and bounce the ball onto the green; or to use my 180-yard-distance-factor 8 wood, which would have cleared the trap by an abundant margin but possibly bounced and rolled well past the pin, even into the rear trap. What I really required to feel confident about the shot was a 9 wood, which would have gotten me about 172 yards of distance. But I didn't yet have one.

Finally I chose my 8 wood. But because of my lingering doubts about overshooting the green, I subconsciously tried to hold back on the shot. The result was a ball that soared offline to the right, putting me in an impossible lie at the very right edge of the trap fronting the green. It took me two strokes to get onto the green from there, and two putts to make a double-bogey 6. Had I had a 9 wood at the time, my hesitancy would have been erased and I would have had a much better chance, psychologically as well as physically, of making the green in regulation on my second shot.

A similar experience befell me on the 170-yard par-3 sixth hole. If I had used my 165-yard 10 wood, I might well have landed my tee shot in the trap guarding the front of the green. Yet my 180-yard 8 wood would probably have bounced over the back of the green and down the steep bank. A 9 wood would have been the ideal club to use here, but I didn't have one. Thinking that I'd be better off in the front trap rather than down the rear bank, but still trying to land on the green, I forced a 10-wood tee shot. The result was another offline shot, this one pulled to the left so that the ball careened off the right-side bank and down into the wooded gorge. I had to chip out from under a tree just to get a decent third shot onto the green, and it took me two putts to make another double-bogey 5.

You can see, then, that when you are playing full-scale woodiron golf, it helps both your confidence and your physical execution to have as many woodirons available as possible. Where, for instance, a clean 10-wood shot may be just a shade too much in distance and roll, a divot 9-iron shot may be the shot you should make—giving you roughly the same distance in the air but less roll once it lands. Or, where a clean 15 wood might be too short and even a divot 12-wood shot too long, a 13- or 14-wood shot might be ideal. As long as you maintain a doubt about any particular shot, the likelihood is that you'll not succeed fully on the shot.

Thus if you are fully committed to woodiron golf by now, your already improved game will benefit even more by gradually, or all at once, adding a 6 and 7 wood, a 9 wood, an 11 wood, and a 13 and 14 wood to your club collection. This, starting from the 5 wood, adds up to a total of 11 clubs. Your driver, 3 wood and putter bring you to your allowable total of 14. If you still wish to carry a regular sand iron for special emergencies, or a favorite shot-chipping iron, you should omit the 14 wood.

Should you decide to add one or more such clubs today, spend part of the morning at the practice range getting used to them, employing the same drills you used for your other woodirons.

The next most common weakness of your round of yesterday was likely your play around the greens with your 15 wood. Surely you muffed a short, straight chip or two, probably a short, high cut shot or two, and no doubt a short shot or two out of traps or deep rough.

Don't despair. These shots are the "touch" shots of the woodiron game, and it takes time and practice to master their touch—by which I mean the force, arc, and type of swing you should use. These factors are almost always dictated by the lie of the ball on any given shot. Yesterday you encountered some lies you hadn't been faced with in your previous rounds and practice-tee sessions.

Your task now is continually to improve your touch on any short around-the-green shot you may have to make. You should begin by spending part of your morning—an hour or so—practicing the entire variety of such shots at several different greens scattered around your course. Work out of every different kind of lie imaginable, from deep, level rough and sand to steep banks and hardpan, from green fringe grass to thin rough, from levels below the greens to levels above them. Concentrate all the while on putting each shot as close to the pin as possible.

The third major weakness you probably manifested during yesterday's practice round was a tendency to have difficulty with your woodiron shots from slanted lies—uphill, downhill, sidehill. Solving this is another matter of putting in more work. Once again, go out on your course and spend half an hour hitting 5-, 10-, and 15-wood shots from such lies. Work on getting your basic woodiron stance and address right for each type of lie, and on keeping your swing force and tempo properly grooved.

When you have completed these "reassessment" drills, you will be ready for a final exam, so to speak, leading to your graduation. The final exam will take the form of one last practice round this afternoon, using all the woodirons you have so far collected, before you start playing competitive golf again.

19

The seventh day: afternoon session

Your goal this afternoon is to better your performance of yesterday by at least three strokes, exploiting what you learned this morning about correcting your major weaknesses. Again, preplay your round on paper and make sure you take a complete and proper warm-up session before you approach the first tee. And again, focus your concentration more sharply on the woodiron principles symbolized by our cryptic motto: TEFOLCO. Indeed, don't hesitate to write it on the back of your own hand and consult it before each shot.

As you have done previously, play a few holes with me over the Links one last time. This time I'm not going to describe my own play. Instead we'll follow three other golfers—one a long hitter, the second a medium hitter, the third a short hitter—and see how each plays the course using full woodiron sets.

I will call the three golfers Long, Medium, and Short. Until he switched over to woodirons, Long played to a handicap of 15. Medium's handicap was 20 before he switched. Short's impost was 25. Long's full-out driving distance was a wild 260 yards, but now he settles for a consistently straight 230. Medium's was 230 yards; and he now is happy with 215. Short's was 200 yards, but because he wasn't as wild, he has had to reduce his distance by only 10 yards, to 190, to achieve consistent accuracy. Each golfer hits his ascending-numbered woods proportionately shorter distances.

Let's pick them up at the par-3 190-yard fifteenth hole and follow them to the end of their round. So far their scores are:

Hole	Long	Medium	Short	Par
1	4	5	5	4
2	4	4	4	4
3	5	5	5	4
4	5	5	5	4
5	5	6	5	5
6	4	3	3	3
7	5	6	6	5
8	4	4	5	4
9	3	3	4	3
10	5	4	5	4
11	3	4	4	3
12	4	5	5	4
13	5	5	5	5
14	4	4	5	4
Total	**60**	**63**	**66**	**56**

As you can see, through the Links' fourteenth hole *Long* is playing at just four over par, while *Medium* is seven over and *Short* is ten over—vast improvements for each when compared to what they'd be shooting on the basis of their old handicaps. Depending on your own realistic controlled-driving distance, put yourself in the place of either *Long, Medium,* or *Short* as they finish out the last four holes.

Fifteenth Hole: Par 3: 190 yards
Long: Tee shot with his 8 wood bounced two yards in front of green and rolled to a stop 18 feet from cup. Two putts for a *par 3.*

Medium: Tee shot with his 5 wood faded slightly right and landed in front-right trap, medium deep. Second shot, a 15-wood cut blast, put him on green 16 feet from cup. Two putts for a *bogey 4*.

Short: Laid up tee shot in front of fairway trap with his 9 wood. Second shot a 15-wood choke-grip divot pitch of 40 yards to within 5 feet of cup. One putt for a *par 3*.

Sixteenth Hole: Par 4: 400 yards
Long: Tee shot with driver stopped dead center 220 yards out in slightly uphill fairway. Second shot, 180 yards farther uphill to green, made with his 8 wood, stopped left forefront of green 30 feet from cup. Three putts for a *bogey 5*.

Medium: Tee shot with driver drifted wide into center of shallow driving trap on right 200 yards out. Hit a 6-wood second shot from firm sand lie 160 yards toward green. Third shot an uphill half-swing 15-wood pitch that landed on green and stopped 6 feet from cup. Two putts for a *bogey 5*.

Short: Tee shot with driver 180 yards out and dead center. With 220 yards to go, hit second shot with his 3 wood 170 yards farther up fairway, leaving himself with a 50-yard approach. Hit green on third shot with a full-swing half-choke straight 15-wood pitch. Two putts for a score of *bogey 5*.

Seventeenth Hole: Par 5: 480 yards
Long: Slightly downhill tee shot 230 yards to left center of fairway; ball rolled into fringe of low rough at fairway's edge 30 yards in front of brook. With a good angle around dogleg, hit second shot with 5 wood 200 yards to right side of fairway, just ahead of trap in crook of fairway. Third shot, a 50-yard 15-wood half-swing pitch, carried a bit far, however, putting Long in the deep trap encircling the left side of grass. A powerful cut blast got him out and onto the green and two putts gave him a score of *bogey 5*.

Medium: Tee shot with driver landed on right side of fairway 215 yards out and 45 yards from brook. Second shot, a straight 200-yard

3 wood, put him out ahead of the dogleg on the extreme left side of fairway, facing a 165-yard approach to the green. He made this with his 8 wood, but in an attempt to avoid the curling trap around the left front of the green, he carried the ball wide to the right and into the right-hand trap. Out in four and two putts for a *bogey 6.*

Short: Tee shot with driver 190 yards out in midfairway. A 3-wood straight second shot carried over the brook and stopped 175 yards farther down fairway on right, near crook trap. Third shot called for Short to loft his ball over protruding edge of trap toward green's open front, a distance of 120 yards to the green. He struck a perfect clean 10 wood and landed the ball 4 yards in front of the green, bouncing and rolling it up to within 3 feet of pin. Holed out in one putt for a *birdie 3.*

Eighteenth Hole: Par 4: 410 yards
Long: Tee shot with driver landed left center of fairway, well beyond left driving trap at 230 yards. Second shot of 180 yards steeply uphill to green really played at 200 to 210 yards, so Long hit a 6 wood to get over brook and lay up to a distance of 20 yards from green. Third shot a 15-wood uphill cut chip to within 8 feet of pin. Two putts for a *bogey 5.*

Medium: Tee shot with driver split the fairway traps and stopped 210 yards from tee and 200 from green. Used his 3-wood to carry across pond and lay up 40 yards from green. Hit straight uphill 15 wood as a low pitch; it hit fairway shoulder in front of elevated green and rolled on. Two putts for a *bogey 5.*

Short: Tee shot of 180 yards drifted right and caught big, shallow driving trap. Hit a 14 wood 90 yards out of trap to lay up in front of brook. Third shot over brook and uphill to elevated green, was a 130-yarder that played like 150 yards. Short hit an 8 wood that soared onto green and stopped 20 feet from cup. Two putts for a *bogey 5.*

Now let's look at the three players' final scores. Long added a par 3 and three bogey 5s to his 60 after 14 holes for a total of 78—6 over par. Medium added a bogey 4, 5, 6, and 5 to his 63 for a total of 83—11 over par. And Short added two 3s and two 5s to his 14-hole score of 66 for a total of 82—10 over par.

When you consider that their previous handicaps with conventional irons were, respectively, 15, 20, and 25, this was a remarkable performance for each. Whereas Long used to score regularly around 87, now he could play at 78. Medium played regularly at around 92; now he could score 83. The most remarkable of all was Short. Once a regular 97–98 player, he came in on this round with an 82—a score that represented a reduction of more than half his handicap when he played with conventional irons.

Take this lesson to heart, all you high handicappers, as you go out to play your final practice round. No, you won't suddenly play scratch golf. But by concentrating on the principles of the woodiron game, you too can cut your present handicap in half.

796.352 Kiernan, Thomas
KIE
        Woodirons

DATE			
SEP 19			
OCT 3			
MAY 24			
MAY 11			
APR			
MAY 23			

© THE BAKER & TAYLOR CO.